하루 30분, 영어 문해력이 자라는 신문 읽기의 힘

바빠 영어 신문

NEWS TIMES

뉴스 타임스

환경·과학

이지스에듀

지은이 | 성기홍(효린파파)

EBS English 대표 강사이자 효린파파e어학원 대표이다. 13년 동안 중·고등학교에서 영어를 가르친 전직 교사이이도 하다. 효린·이준 두 아이의 아빠로서 아이들이 영어에 푹 빠져서 정말 영어를 잘하게 되는 환경을 탐구하고 실천하고 있으며, 이렇게 터득한 영어 코칭 노하우를 '효린파파' 인스타그램과 유튜브 채널을 통해 아낌없이 공유하고 있다. 아이들에게 시험을 치는 용도가 아닌 현실에서 사용할 수 있는 진짜 영어 실력을 키워 주기 위해 《바빠 영어신문 NEW TIMES - 사회·경제 편》, 《바빠 초등 영어 일기 쓰기》를 집필했다.
 • 인스타그램 @hyorin_papa2 • 유튜브 youtube.com/@hyorinpapa

지은이 | 송수영

세인트폴 루터란 고등학교(Saint Paul Lutheran High School)를 기처 미국 UC 어바인(University of California, Irvine)에서 의공학(Biomedical Engineering) 학사 및 석사를 마쳤고, 이후 실리콘밸리에서 글로벌 헬스케어 기업 보스턴 사이언티픽(Boston Scientific)에서 제조 엔지니어로 근무했다. 이공계 기반의 논리적 사고력과 영어 실무 경험을 바탕으로, 현재 효린파파e 영어연구소에서 영어 교육 콘텐츠 개발과 학습서 집필에 집중하고 있다.

감수 | Michael A. Putlack (마이클 A. 푸틀랙)

미국의 명문 대학인 Tufts University에서 역사학 석사 학위를 받은 뒤 우리나라의 동양미래대학에서 20년 넘게 한국 학생들을 가르쳤다. 폭넓은 교육 경험을 기반으로 『미국 교과서 읽는 리딩』 같은 어린이 영어 교재를 집필했을 뿐만 아니라 『영어동화 100편』 시리즈, 『7살 첫 영어 - 파닉스』, 『바빠 초등 필수 영단어』 등의 영어 교재 감수에 참여해 오고 있다.

하루 30분, 영어 문해력이 자라는 신문 읽기의 힘

바빠 영어신문 NEW TIMES – 환경·과학 편

초판 1쇄 발행 2025년 10월 10일
초판 2쇄 발행 2025년 12월 15일
지은이 성기홍(효린파파), 송수영　　**원어민 감수** Michael A. Putlack (마이클 A. 푸틀랙)
발행인 이지연
펴낸곳 이지스퍼블리싱(주)　　**제조국명** 대한민국
출판사 등록번호 제313-2010-123호
주소 서울시 마포구 잔다리로 109 이지스 빌딩 5층(우편번호 04003)
대표전화 02-325-1722　　　　　　　　**팩스** 02-326-1723
이지스퍼블리싱 홈페이지 www.easyspub.com　　**이지스에듀 카페** www.easysedu.co.kr
바빠 아지트 블로그 blog.naver.com/easyspub　　**인스타그램** @easys_edu
페이스북 www.facebook.com/easyspub2014　　**이메일** service@easyspub.co.kr

기획 및 책임 편집 이지혜 | 김경진, 박지연, 김현주　　**교정교열** 안현진　　**문제 검수** 이지은
표지 및 내지 디자인 김세리　　**조판** 김민정　　**인쇄** 미래피앤피　　**독자지원** 박애림, 이세진
영업 및 문의 이주동, 김요한(support@easyspub.co.kr)　　**마케팅** 라혜주

ISBN 979-11-6303-767-5 63740
가격 16,800원

• **이지스에듀**는 이지스퍼블리싱(주)의 교육 브랜드입니다.
 (이지스에듀는 학생들을 탈락시키지 않고 모두 목적지까지 데려가는 책을 만듭니다!)

펑펑 쏟아져야 눈이 쌓이듯, 공부도 집중해야 실력이 쌓인다.

학교 선생님부터 영어 전문 명강사들까지
적극 추천한 '바빠 영어 신문 NEWS TIMES'

아이들의 눈높이에 딱 맞는 영어 신문!

이 교재는 아이들에게 부담스럽지 않은 난이도로 지문이 구성되어 있습니다. 한 기사당 총 4단계로 체계적인 학습을 유도합니다. 독해의 기본적인 내용 이해와 어휘 학습뿐 아니라 올바른 작문과 간단한 토론까지 전반적으로 실력을 다질 수 있습니다.

이 책은 아이들의 영어 실력뿐 아니라 사고의 깊이를 더할 수 있도록 도와줄 것입니다.

이은지 선생님
前 (주)탑클래스에듀아이 영어 강사

다양한 언어 능력을 키울 수 있는 책!

신문과 뉴스에서 다루고 있는 다양하고 흥미로운 주제를 영어로 읽음으로써 어휘력 및 독해 실력 향상을 기대할 수 있고, 빈칸 넣기와 문장 쓰기를 통해 영어 글쓰기 능력도 향상시킬 수 있습니다.

더불어 세상에 대한 이해를 넓힐 수 있으며, 글을 읽은 후 부모님과 함께 서로 의견을 주고받는 시간을 가진다면 글을 이해하는 능력과 비판적 사고력도 기를 수 있을 것입니다.

어션 선생님
기초 영어 강사, '어션영어 BasicEnglish' 유튜브 운영자

영어 문해력을 높이는 신문 읽기!

AI시대 미래 인재에게 필수적인 정보 분석력, 비판적 문제 해결력, 창의적 소통 역량을 기를 수 있습니다.

또한 지문 이해, 문장 구성·글쓰기, 세부 정보 파악, 주제별 토론을 통한 표현력 향상까지 단계별 과정을 통해 균형 잡힌 영어 문해력을 향상할 수 있는 교재입니다.

서지예 선생님
부산 공립 중학교 영어교사 겸 작가, '에듀체리' 유튜브 운영자

영어 실력 향상뿐만 아니라 사고 확장까지!

이 교재는 사회, 경제의 중요한 개념이 담긴 주제의 글을 읽으면서, 자연스럽게 영어 어휘력도 키우고, 세상에 대한 관심과 이해도도 높일 수 있도록 설계되어 있습니다. 특히 STEP 4 〈토론하기〉 활동에서는 관련 주제를 다시 한번 생각해 보고, 여러 입장의 의견을 접해 보면서 공감 능력과 생각을 확장할 수 있는 경험을 할 수 있습니다. 이를 바탕으로 자신의 생각을 나타내는 글까지 쓸 수 있겠어요!

김현숙 선생님
영어 강사, '바빠 초등 영어 리딩' 저자

영어 읽기의 폭이 넓어진다!
《바빠 영어 신문 NEWS TIMES》

원어민이 진짜 쓰는 영어를 접할 수 있어요!

이 책은 영어 교과서나 단어장보다 더 현실적이고 생생한 영어 표현을 배울 수 있어요. 신문 기사에는 우리가 현실 세계에서 자주 쓰는 단어나 문장이 많이 나오거든요. 그래서 진짜 사용하는 영어를 접할 수 있죠!

영어 실력 향상과 배경지식 축적을 동시에!

신문 기사는 어휘, 독해, 영작, 회화를 통합적으로 학습하게 해 줍니다. 영어 신문을 꾸준히 읽으면 자연스럽게 영어 실력이 어휘력, 독해력 등 다양한 영역에서 좋아지고, 긴 글도 부담 없이 읽게 돼요. 게다가 다양한 주제(경제, 사회, 환경, 과학 등)의 기사를 읽으면서 배경지식과 시사 상식도 키울 수 있습니다.

쓸 수 있으면 정확히 이해한 거죠!

눈으로만 읽고 끝낸다면, 지문을 온전히 다 이해했다고 보기 힘들 것입니다. 하나를 읽더라도 제대로 읽고 오래 기억할 수 있도록 이 책은 지문을 읽고 문제를 푼 후, 다시 우리말에 맞게 영어 문장을 쓰도록 구성되어 있습니다. 내가 직접 문장을 쓸 수 있다면 그 문장을 정확히 이해한 것이죠!

또 문장을 논리적으로 정리해서 쓸 수 있도록 구성되어 있어서 글의 구성을 보는 감각도 키울 수 있습니다.

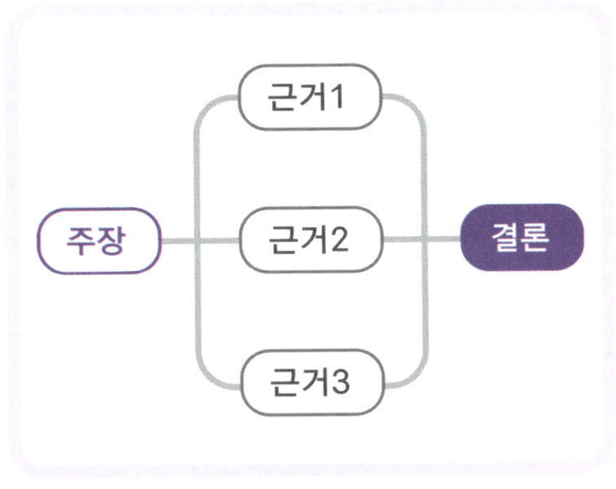

▲ 《바빠 영어 신문 NEWS TIMES》의 논리적인 지문 구성

'4단계 학습법'으로 영어 신문을 완벽히 흡수할 수 있어요!

영어 신문 읽기가 막막하고 두려운 친구들이라면 이 책의 '4단계 학습법'으로 체계적으로 공부하길 추천합니다!

1단계 기사 읽기

영어 신문을 초등학생이 읽을 수 있는 기사로 재구성했어요. 같은 단어가 기사 내에서 반복해서 나오기 때문에 자연스럽게 단어를 익힐 수 있어요. 또 스스로 기사를 읽고 이해할 수 있다는 성취감도 생겨요.

2단계 확인하기

STEP 1에서는 기사를 잘 이해했는지 문제를 제공하고 있어요. 1번 문제는 단어 문제, 2번 문제는 내용의 일치&불일치 문제, 3번 문제는 한 줄 요약 문제로 영어 문해력을 키울 수 있어요.

3단계 기사 쓰기

STEP 2에서는 앞에서 학습한 기사를 떠올리며 한 문장씩 직접 써요. 기사처럼 논리적인 글쓰기를 훈련할 수 있어요! 혹시 어렵다면 앞 쪽으로 돌아가서 확인하며 진행해도 좋아요.

4단계 정리&토론

STEP 3에서는 앞에서 학습한 기사를 요약해서 '주장-근거-결론'으로 다시 정리해요. 그 다음, STEP 4에서는 주제에 대한 찬성과 반대를 생각할 수 있는 토론 학습이 있어요!

TIP

'오늘부터 30일 동안 영어 신문을 읽을 거야!'라고 공개적으로 약속하면 끝까지 할 확률이 높아진대요! 결심과 함께 책 사진을 찍어 친구나 부모님께 공유해 보세요!

바빠 영어신문 NEWS TIMES – 환경·과학 편

📅 공부한 날

1단계 | 신문 읽기

세 번 이상 읽어요!

1회: 눈으로 읽기
2회: 원어민 음원을 들으며 읽기
3회: 큰 소리로 읽기

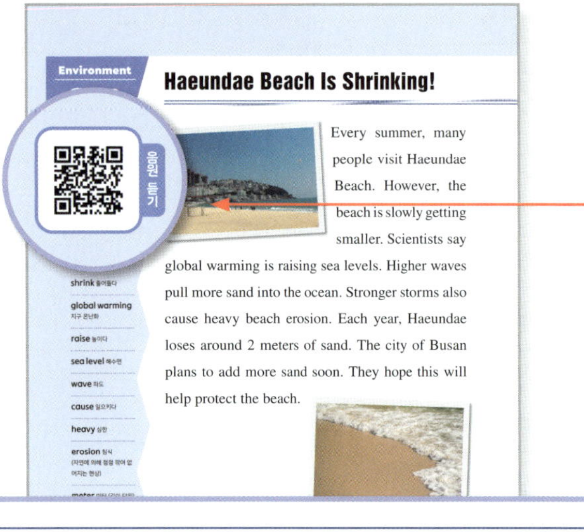

QR코드를 찍으면
원어민 음원을 들을 수 있어요.

2021년 조사에 따르면, 해운대의 하얀 모래가 20% 넘게 줄었다고 해요. 특히 여름철에는 파도가 더 거세져서, 모래를 바다로 훨씬 많이 가져간다고 해요. 그래서 부산시는 해변을 보호하기 위해 매년 수억 원을 들여 모래를 다시 채우고 있어요. 친구들이라면 해운대를 지키기 위해 어떤 새로운 아이디어를 내보고 싶나요?

오늘의 지문을 더 잘 이해할 수
있도록 추가 정보를 읽을 수 있어요.

2단계 | 확인하기

세 번 이상 읽었으면 문제를 풀어요!

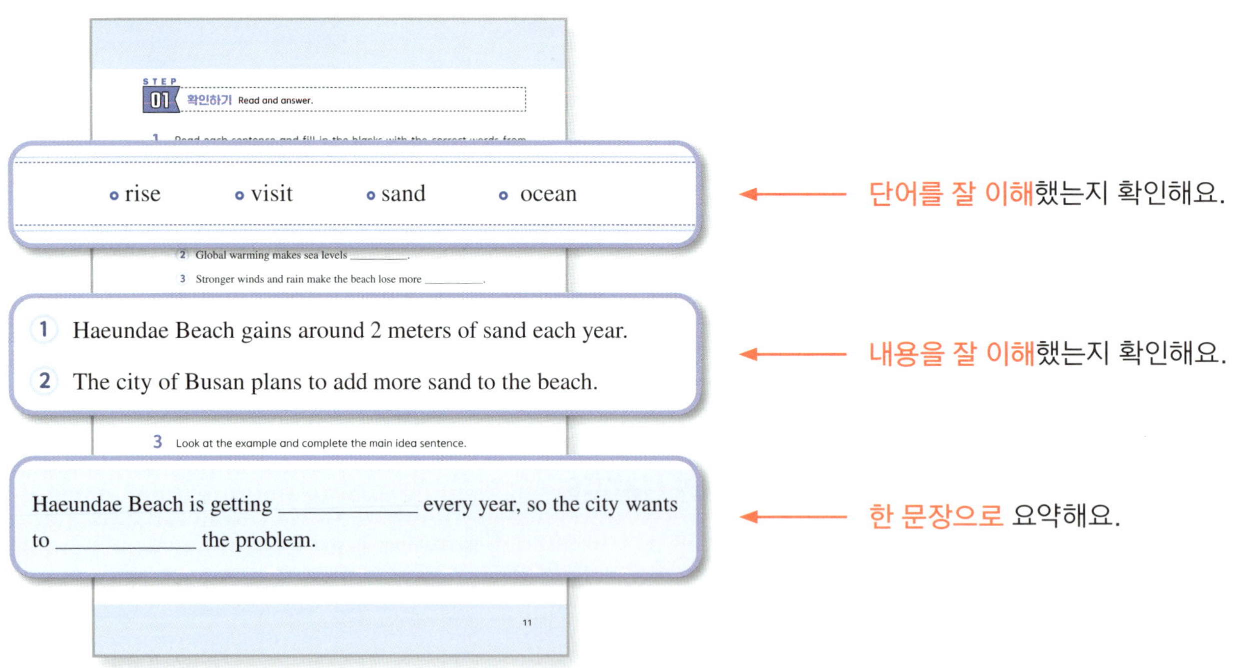

단어를 잘 이해했는지 확인해요.

내용을 잘 이해했는지 확인해요.

한 문장으로 요약해요.

영어 문장력을 키워요!

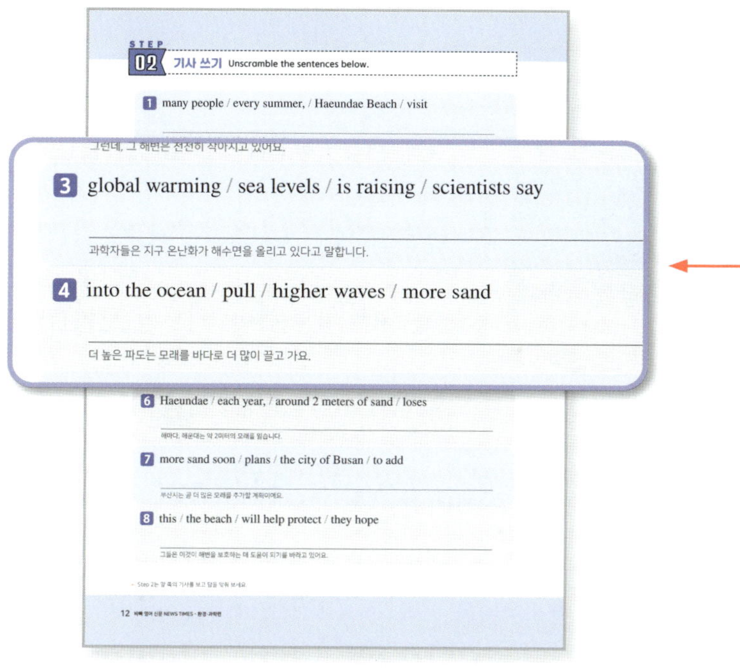

해석을 보며 **영어 작문**을 해 보세요.
어려우면 앞 쪽의 기사를
보고 와도 좋아요.

사고력, 논리력을 키워요!

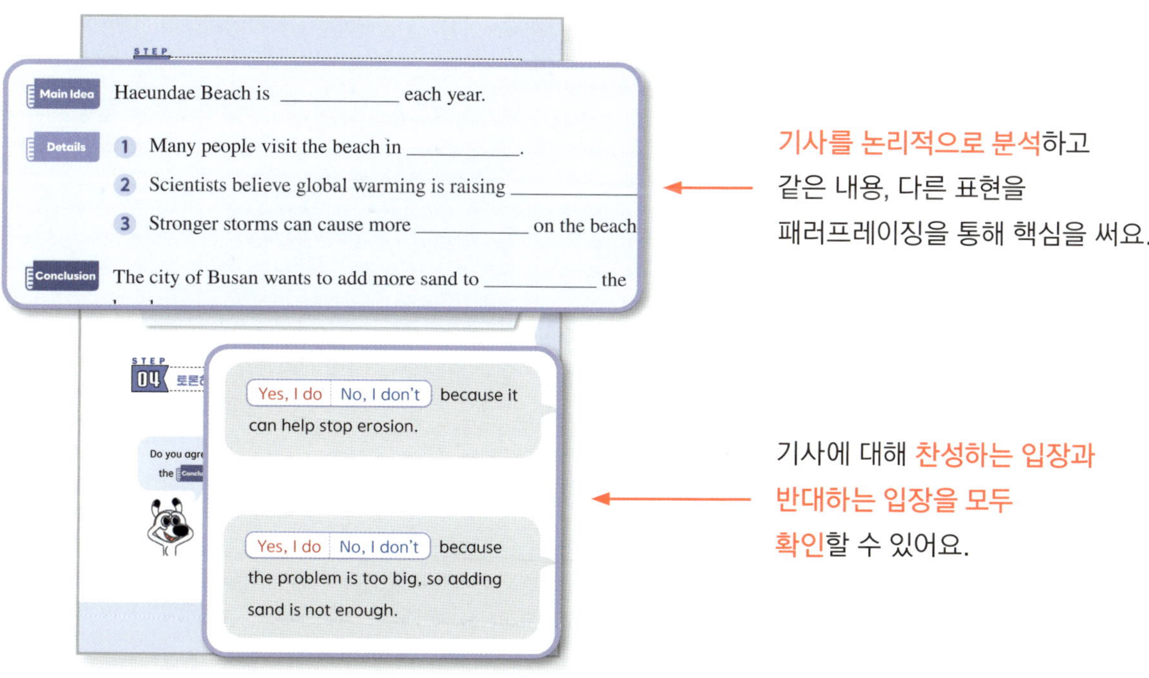

기사를 논리적으로 분석하고
같은 내용, 다른 표현을
패러프레이징을 통해 핵심을 써요.

기사에 대해 **찬성하는 입장**과
반대하는 입장을 모두
확인할 수 있어요.

Haeundae Beach Is Shrinking!

Every summer, many people visit Haeundae Beach. However, the beach is slowly getting smaller. Scientists say global warming is raising sea levels. Higher waves pull more sand into the ocean. Stronger storms also cause heavy beach erosion. Each year, Haeundae loses around 2 meters of sand. The city of Busan plans to add more sand soon. They hope this will help protect the beach.

Word Bank

shrink 줄어들다

global warming 지구 온난화

raise 높이다

sea level 해수면

wave 파도

cause 일으키다

heavy 심한

erosion 침식 (자연에 의해 점점 깎여 없어지는 현상)

meter 미터 (길이 단위)

protect 보호하다

⭐ 2021년 조사에 따르면, 해운대의 하얀 모래가 20% 넘게 줄었다고 해요. 특히 여름철에는 파도가 더 거세져서, 모래를 바다로 훨씬 많이 가져간다고 해요. 그래서 부산시는 해변을 보호하기 위해 매년 수억 원을 들여 모래를 다시 채우고 있어요. 친구들이라면 해운대를 지키기 위해 어떤 새로운 아이디어를 내보고 싶나요?

1 Fill in the blanks with the correct words from the box. One word will not be used.

1 A lot of people ____________ Haeundae Beach every summer.

2 Global warming makes sea levels ____________.

3 Stronger winds and rain make the beach lose more ____________.

2 After reading the article, circle **T**(true) or **F**(false).

1 Haeundae Beach gains around 2 meters of sand each year. T F

2 The city of Busan plans to add more sand to the beach. T F

❋ gain 얻다

3 Complete the main idea sentence with words from the box.

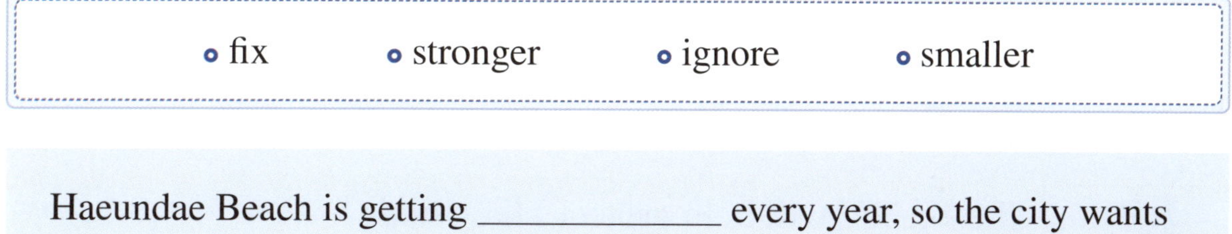

Haeundae Beach is getting ____________ every year, so the city wants to ____________ the problem.

❋ fix 고치다   ignore 무시하다

1 many people / every summer, / Haeundae Beach / visit

매년 여름, 많은 사람들이 해운대 해변을 방문해요.

2 is slowly getting / the beach / however, / smaller

그런데, 그 해변은 천천히 작아지고 있어요.

3 global warming / sea levels / is raising / scientists say

과학자들은 지구 온난화가 해수면을 올리고 있다고 말합니다.

4 into the ocean / pull / higher waves / more sand

더 높은 파도는 모래를 바다로 더 많이 끌고 가요.

5 heavy / also cause / stronger storms / beach erosion

더 강한 폭풍 또한 심한 해변 침식을 일으켜요.

6 Haeundae / each year, / around 2 meters of sand / loses

해마다, 해운대는 약 2미터의 모래를 잃습니다.

7 more sand soon / plans / the city of Busan / to add

부산시는 곧 더 많은 모래를 추가할 계획이에요.

8 this / the beach / will help protect / they hope

그들은 이것이 해변을 보호하는 데 도움이 되기를 바라고 있어요.

← Step 2는 앞 쪽의 기사를 보고 답을 맞춰 보세요.

정리하기 Choose a word from the box and complete the organizer.

- protect
- shrinking
- erosion
- sea levels
- winter
- summer

Main Idea Haeundae Beach is ______________ each year.

Details

1. Many people visit the beach in ____________.
2. Scientists believe global warming is raising ______________.
3. Stronger storms can cause more ____________ on the beach.

Conclusion The city of Busan wants to add more sand to ____________ the beach.

STEP
04

토론하기 Choose and circle the correct answers.

Word Bank

screen (time)
화면 (보는 시간)

blue light 블루라이트
(전자기기 화면에서 나오는
파란빛)

hormone 호르몬

melatonin 멜라토닌

in fact 실제, 사실상

reduce 감소시키다

poor 좋지 못한

expert 전문가

habit 습관

Sleep Better with Less Screen Time

These days, kids often watch videos or play games before bed. Blue light from screens makes the brain think it is daytime. This happens because it lowers a sleep hormone called melatonin. In fact, blue light before bedtime can reduce melatonin by 55%. Less melatonin makes it harder to fall asleep at night. Poor sleep can cause mood and health problems. Experts say to stop looking at screens one hour before bed. This simple habit can lead to better sleep.

⭐ 한 연구에 따르면, 잠들기 1시간 전에 스마트폰을 보면 평균 30분 정도 늦게 잠든다고 해요. 어떤 친구들은 "눈은 피곤한데도 잠이 안 와요"라고 말하기도 했어요. 그건 뇌가 화면의 밝은 빛 때문에 아직도 낮이라고 착각하고 있기 때문일 수 있다고 해요. 친구들은 뇌에게 "이제 잘 시간이야"라고 알려주려면, 어떤 좋은 습관을 가져야 한다고 생각하나요?

1 Fill in the blanks with the correct words from the box. One word will not be used.

> ○ screens   ○ health   ○ bedtime   ○ games

(1) Kids now often watch videos or play ___________ before bed.

(2) Blue light from ___________ can make kids feel awake at night.

(3) Poor sleep is bad for their ___________ and moods.

2 After reading the article, circle **T**(true) or **F**(false).

(1) Experts say kids should stop using screens at least 12 hours before bed.   T F

(2) Less melatonin makes it harder for kids to sleep.   T F

3 Complete the main idea sentence with words from the box.

> ○ pattern   ○ hormone   ○ difficult   ○ habit

Watching screens at night can lower the sleep ___________ and make sleeping at night more ___________.

✳ pattern 패턴

1 often watch videos / kids / before bed / or play games / these days,

요즘, 아이들은 자기 전에 자주 영상을 보거나 게임을 합니다.

2 think / makes / it is daytime / the brain / blue light from screens

화면에서 나오는 블루라이트는 뇌가 낮이라고 생각하게 만들어요.

3 called melatonin / lowers / it / a sleep hormone / because / this happens

이것은 그것(블루라이트)이 멜라토닌이라는 수면 호르몬을 줄이기 때문에 발생해요.

4 can reduce / blue light before bedtime / by 55% / melatonin / in fact,

사실, 잠자기 전 블루라이트는 멜라토닌을 55%까지 줄일 수 있어요.

5 makes it harder / at night / to fall asleep / less melatonin

더 적은 멜라토닌은 밤에 잠드는 것을 더 어렵게 만들어요.

6 mood and health problems / can cause / poor sleep

부족한 수면은 기분과 건강 문제를 일으킬 수 있어요.

7 to stop / experts say / one hour / looking at screens / before bed

전문가들은 잠자기 한 시간 전에는 화면을 보지 말라고 말해요.

8 lead to / better sleep / can / this simple habit

이렇게 간단한 습관이 더 나은 잠으로 이어질 수 있답니다.

← Step 2는 앞 쪽의 기사를 보고 답을 맞춰 보세요.

- raises
- blue
- poor
- daytime
- reduces
- bed

Main Idea ______________ light before bed can hurt kids' sleep.

Details

1. Blue light makes the brain think it is ________________.
2. It ______________ melatonin levels, which can make it hard for kids to sleep.
3. ____________ sleep quality can cause mood and health problems.

Conclusion That's why experts say to stop watching screens before ____________.

※ (sleep) quality (수면의) 질

STEP 04 토론하기 Choose and circle the correct answers.

Do you agree with the **Conclusion** ?

※ awake 깨어 있는

When Cows Burp, the Earth Gets Hot

Word Bank

burp 트림하다

beef 소고기

popular 인기 있는

raise (cows)
(소를) 키우다

methane 메탄 가스
(지구를 뜨겁게 하는 기체)

heat 덥게 만들다

research 연구

produce
생산하다, 만들다

solve 해결하다

seaweed
(미역, 다시마 등의) 해초

Beef is a popular choice for meat around the world. But raising cows hurts the Earth when they burp. The gas from these burps is called methane, and it heats the Earth. Research shows cows produce about 100 kilograms of methane each year. One way to solve the problem is to change the cows' food. Adding special plants like seaweed helps cows burp less. Another way is to eat less beef and meat. These small changes can help protect the Earth.

소 한 마리가 1년에 내뿜는 메탄은 약 100kg 정도인데, 이 양은 자동차로 4,000km를 달릴 때 나오는 온실가스와 비슷하다고 해요. 전 세계에는 이런 소가 10억 마리 넘게 살고 있어서, 지구의 기후에 미치는 영향이 생각보다 훨씬 크다고 해요. 친구들이라면 소가 내뿜는 메탄을 줄이기 위해 어떤 아이디어를 떠올려볼 수 있을까요?

1 Fill in the blanks with the correct words from the box. One word will not be used.

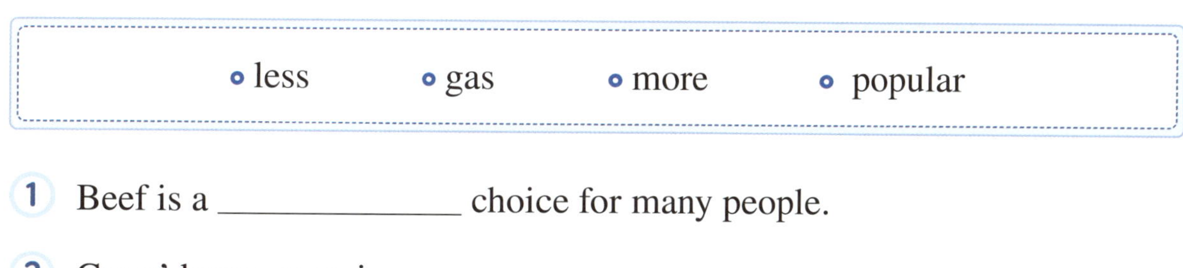

1 Beef is a ______________ choice for many people.

2 Cows' burps contain a ___________.

3 Small changes like eating ___________ beef can help the problem.

2 After reading the article, circle **T**(true) or **F**(false).

1 Cows make just a small amount of methane each year.   T F

2 Adding seaweed to cow food can help reduce gas.   T F

※ amount 양

3 Complete the main idea sentence with words from the box.

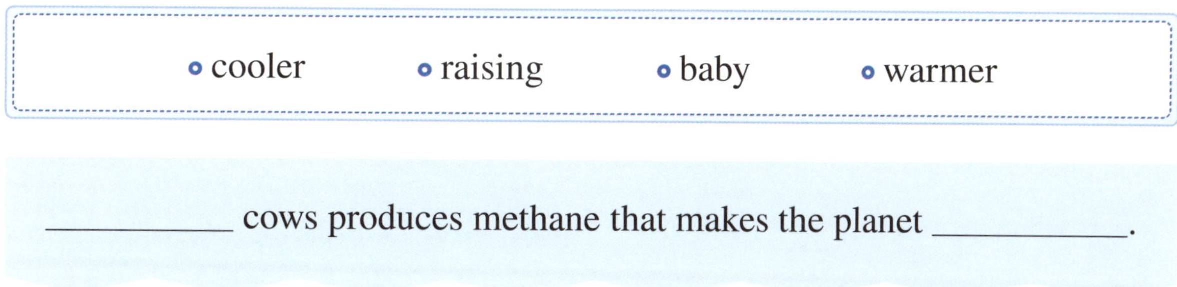

___________ cows produces methane that makes the planet ___________.

※ planet 행성

1 is / beef / a popular choice / around the world / for meat

____

소고기는 전 세계에서 고기로서 인기 있는 선택이에요.

2 when they burp / hurts / raising cows / the Earth / but

____

그런데 소를 기르는 것은 그들이 트림할 때 지구를 해치게 해요.

3 from these burps / the gas / and it heats the Earth / is called methane,

____

이 트림에서 나오는 가스는 메탄이라고 불리며, 이것은 지구를 덥게 만듭니다.

4 each year / produce / cows / about 100 kilograms of methane

Research shows
____

연구는 소들은 매년 약 100킬로그램의 메탄을 만든다는 것을 보여줘요.

5 to solve the problem / one way / is / the cows' food / to change

____

이 문제를 해결하는 한 가지 방법은 소들의 먹이를 바꾸는 것입니다.

6 like seaweed / adding special plants / cows burp / helps / less

____

해조류 같은 특별한 식물들을 더하면 소들이 트림을 덜 하도록 도와줘요.

7 is / beef and meat / less / to eat / another way

____

또 다른 방법은 소고기와 고기를 덜 먹는 거예요.

8 protect / can help / the Earth / these small changes

____

이런 작은 변화들이 지구를 보호하는 데 도움이 될 수 있어요.

← Step 2는 앞 쪽의 기사를 보고 답을 맞춰 보세요.

정리하기 Choose a word from the box and complete the organizer.

> ○ beef   ○ diet   ○ harmful
> ○ chicken   ○ heats   ○ protect

**Main Idea** Raising cows adds a ______________ gas to the air.

**Details**

1. This gas is called methane, and it __________ the Earth.

2. However, changing their __________ may help them produce less gas.

3. Eating less __________ can also help.

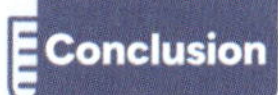**Conclusion** Changing the diet of both cows and people can help __________ the planet.

※ diet 식단   harmful 해로운

토론하기 Choose and circle the correct answers.

Do you agree with the **Detail 3** ?

Can We Find Life Beyond Earth?

Many people wonder if life exists beyond Earth. NASA sends robots to explore space and to look for signs of life. Right now, NASA is exploring Mars the most. In 2021, NASA sent a robot called Perseverance to Mars. After studying Mars, NASA wants to explore more places. One place that NASA is interested in is Europa, a moon of Jupiter. Scientists believe water under Europa's ice may have life. Finding life would be a very important moment for science.

Word Bank

beyond ~ 너머에

wonder 궁금해하다

if ~인지 아닌지

exist 존재하다

explore 탐험하다, 탐사하다

sign 징후, 신호

Mars 화성

be interested in ~에 관심이 있다

moon 위성

Jupiter 목성

moment 순간

☆ '퍼서비어런스(Perseverance)'는 나사(NASA, 미국 항공우주국)가 2021년에 보낸 화성 탐사 로봇이에요. 유로파(Europa)는 목성을 도는 얼음 위성으로, 얼음 아래에 바다가 숨겨져 있을 수 있다고 해요. NASA는 이 바닷속에 생명체가 살고 있을 가능성에 주목하고 있어요. 그래서 NASA는 2024년에 '유로파 클리퍼'를 발사했고, 2030년에 유로파 근처에 도착할 예정이에요. 친구들은 얼음 밑 깊은 바닷속에서 어떤 생명체가 살고 있을지 상상해 본 적 있나요?

1 Fill in the blanks with the correct words from the box. One word will not be used.

> ○ science   ○ beyond   ○ moon   ○ robots

(1) Many people wonder about life ____________ our planet.

(2) NASA is sending ____________ to search for signs of life in space.

(3) Finding life would be a huge moment for ____________.

2 After reading the article, circle **T**(true) or **F**(false).

(1) In 2021, NASA sent a robot called Perseverance to Mars.   T   F

(2) Scientists think there may be life on the Earth's moon.   T   F

3 Complete the main idea sentence with words from the box.

> ○ Earth   ○ wondering   ○ aliens   ○ exploring

Scientists are ____________ space with robots to find signs of life beyond ____________.

❋ alien 외계인

1 wonder / many people / if life / beyond Earth / exists

____

많은 사람들이 지구 너머에 생명체가 존재하는지 궁금해합니다.

2 signs of life / sends robots / and to look for / to explore space / NASA

____

NASA는 우주를 탐사하고 생명체의 흔적을 찾기 위해 로봇들을 보내요.

3 NASA / right now, / Mars the most / is exploring

____

지금 현재, NASA는 화성을 가장 많이 탐사하고 있어요.

4 NASA / in 2021, / sent / to Mars / a robot called Perseverance

____

2021년에 NASA는 '퍼서비어런스'라는 이름의 로봇을 화성에 보냈어요.

5 NASA / more places / wants to explore / after studying Mars,

____

화성을 연구한 후, NASA는 더 많은 장소들을 탐사하고 싶어 해요.

6 that NASA is interested in / one place / Europa, / is / a moon of Jupiter

____

NASA가 관심을 가지고 있는 장소 중 하나는 목성의 위성인 유로파입니다.

7 water / life / under Europa's ice / scientists believe / may have

____

과학자들은 유로파의 얼음 아래에 있는 물이 생명체를 가지고 있을 수도 있다고 믿어요.

8 would be / finding life / for science / a very important moment

____

생명체를 발견하는 일은 과학에 있어 아주 중요한 순간이 될 거예요.

← Step 2는 앞 쪽의 기사를 보고 답을 맞춰 보세요.

- life
- Europa
- stars
- discovery
- Mars
- sends

Main Idea Scientists are looking for ____________ beyond Earth.

Details
1. NASA ____________ robots into space to explore.
2. A robot called Perseverance went to ____________ in 2021.
3. NASA plans to study ____________, which may have water beneath the ice.

Conclusion Finding life in space would be a huge ____________.

※ discovery 발견   beneath ~ 아래에

Do you agree with the **Main Idea**?

Yes, I do | No, I don't because our planet needs a lot of help, so we should focus on helping the Earth.

Yes, I do | No, I don't because it helps scientists understand how life begins.

※ focus 집중하다

Plant-Based Meat: Good or Bad?

More people want food that is better for our planet. That's why many people now choose plant-based meat. This kind of meat is made from plants, not animals. It uses less water and makes less pollution than animal meat. For example, it uses 90% less water than making real meat. But some people worry that it is not good for our health. It can have too much salt or too many chemicals. Even so, the market for plant-based meat is growing.

요즘엔 식물성 고기를 쓰는 햄버거 가게나 피자 브랜드도 늘고 있어요. 실제로 '버거킹'에서 2019년에 식물성 고기 버거를 출시했을 때, 어느 달에는 이 제품이 기존 소고기 버거보다 더 많이 팔린 기록도 있었다고 해요. 햄버거, 피자 외에 식물성 고기로 만들어 보면 맛있을 것 같은 음식은 뭐가 있을까요?

1 Fill in the blanks with the correct words from the box. One word will not be used.

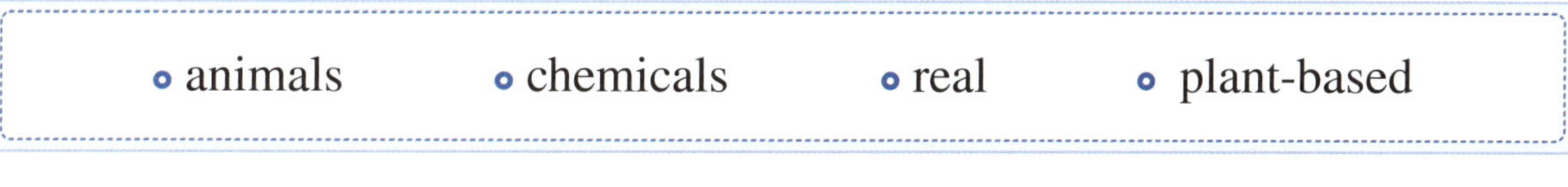

1 ________________ meat helps our planet.

2 Plant-based meat does not come from __________ like cows or pigs.

3 Some people worry it has too many ______________.

2 After reading the article, circle T(true) or F(false).

1 Plant-based meat uses less water and makes less pollution.   T   F

2 Everyone agrees that plant-based meat is perfect.   T   F

3 Complete the main idea sentence with words from the box.

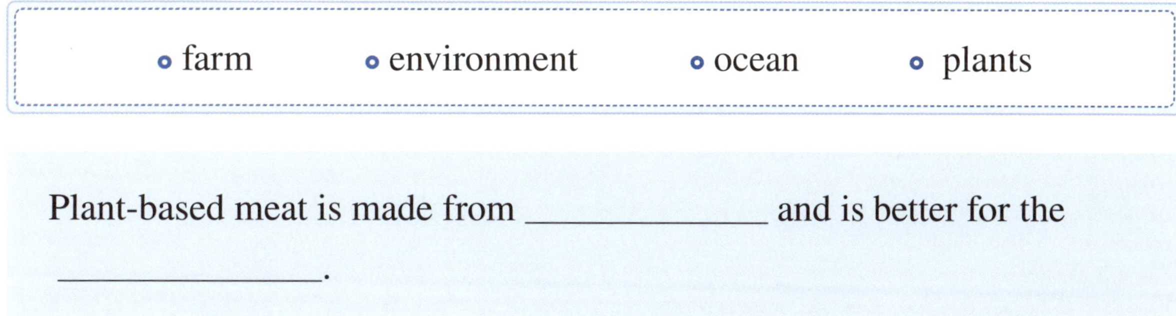

Plant-based meat is made from ______________ and is better for the ______________.

✷ environment 환경

1 want / more people / food / for our planet / that is better

____

더 많은 사람들이 우리 행성(지구)에 더 나은 음식을 원하고 있습니다.

2 many people / that's why / plant-based meat / now choose

____

그렇기 때문에 지금은 많은 사람들이 식물성 고기를 선택해요.

3 is made / not animals / from plants, / this kind of meat

____

이런 종류의 고기는 동물이 아니라 식물로 만들어져요.

4 than animal meat / uses less water / it / and makes less pollution

____

그것은 동물 고기보다 물을 덜 쓰고 오염도 덜 만들어요.

5 uses / it / than making real meat / 90% less water / for example,

____

예를 들어, 그것은 진짜 고기를 만드는 것보다 물을 90% 덜 사용합니다.

6 for our health / some people / but / that it is not good / worry

____

하지만 어떤 사람들은 건강에 안 좋을까 봐 걱정해요.

7 can have / or too many chemicals / too much salt / it

____

소금이나 화학물질이 너무 많을 수도 있거든요.

8 is growing / the market / even so, / for plant-based meat

____

그럼에도 불구하고 식물성 고기 시장은 커지고 있어요.

← Step 2는 앞 쪽의 기사를 보고 답을 맞춰 보세요.

- less
- Earth
- unhealthy
- market
- salt
- more

Main Idea Plant-based meat is better for the ____________ than real meat.

Details

1. It uses less water and makes ____________ pollution.

2. But some people worry it is ____________.

3. It can have too much ____________ or too many chemicals.

Conclusion Still, the ____________ for plant-based meat keeps getting bigger.

※ unhealthy 건강에 해로운

Do you agree with the **Main Idea**?

Yes, I do / No, I don't because plant-based meat does not harm the planet as much.

Yes, I do / No, I don't because plant-based meat is made in factories, which creates pollution.

※ harm 해를 주다   factory 공장

Can a Machine Catch a Lie?

Lie detectors are becoming more common these days. They look at body changes during questions. When people lie or feel nervous, their hearts beat faster. They may also breathe faster and begin to sweat. Police sometimes use lie detectors when asking questions. Some people worry that they are not always right. One study found that lie detectors are wrong about 30% of the time. The machines are smart but still need careful use.

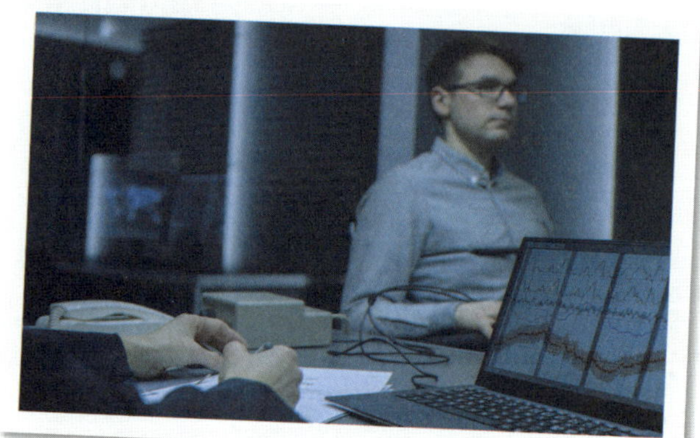

Word Bank

machine 기계

catch 잡아내다

lie detector 거짓말 탐지기

common 흔한

nervous 긴장한

beat (심장이) 뛰다

breathe 숨 쉬다

sweat 땀을 흘리다

study 연구

of the time 전체 시간/경우 중에서

✪ 과학자들은 실험 참가자에게 질문을 하면서 손바닥의 땀과 심장 박동을 측정했다고 해요. 그랬더니 거짓말을 할 때 대부분 땀이 많아지고, 심장도 더 빨리 뛴다는 결과가 나왔어요. 하지만 진실을 말해도 긴장하면 비슷한 반응이 나타날 수 있다는 점도 함께 밝혀졌어요. 친구들은 긴장한 것과 거짓말한 것을 어떻게 구별할 수 있을지 생각해 본 적 있나요?

01 확인하기 Read and answer.

1 Fill in the blanks with the correct words from the box. One word will not be used.

> ○ police　　○ sweat　　○ machine　　○ common

1 Lie detectors are now more ___________ than before.

2 Some people ___________ when they are nervous.

3 ___________ sometimes use lie detectors to ask questions.

2 After reading the article, circle **T**(true) or **F**(false).

1 Sometimes lie detectors give wrong answers.　　T　F

2 When people lie, their hearts usually beat slower.　　T　F

3 Complete the main idea sentence with words from the box.

> ○ help　　○ weight　　○ catch　　○ changes

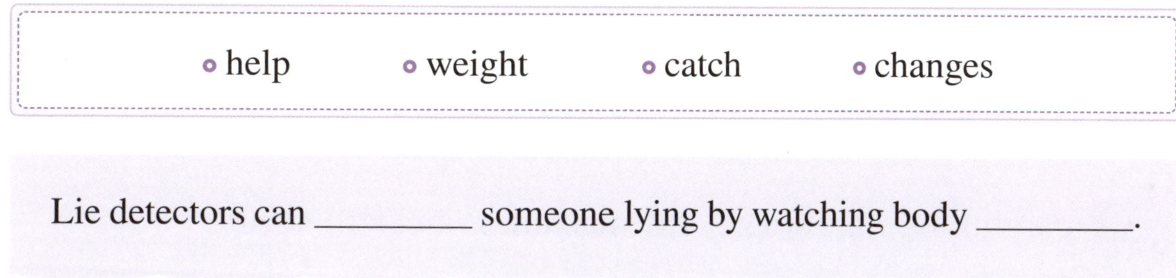

Lie detectors can ___________ someone lying by watching body ___________.

❇ weight 무게

1 are becoming / more common these days / lie detectors

요즘 거짓말 탐지기가 점점 더 흔해지고 있어요.

2 look at / during questions / body changes / they

그것들은 질문들 동안에 몸의 변화들을 봅니다.

3 people lie / when / or feel nervous, / beat faster / their hearts

사람들이 거짓말을 하거나 긴장하면, 그들의 심장은 더 빨리 뛰어요.

4 and begin to sweat / may also breathe / they / faster

그들은 또한 숨을 더 빨리 쉬거나 땀을 흘리기 시작할 수도 있어요.

5 asking questions / sometimes use lie detectors / police / when

경찰은 때때로 질문할 때 거짓말 탐지기들을 사용해요.

6 worry / some people / always right / that they are not

어떤 사람들은 그것들이 항상 옳지는 않다고 걱정해요.

7 are wrong / of the time / about 30% / lie detectors / one study found that

한 연구는 거짓말 탐지기가 전체 경우 중에서 약 30%는 틀리다는 것을 발견했어요.

8 careful use / are smart / the machines / but still need

기계들은 똑똑하지만, 여전히 신중한 사용을 필요로 합니다.

← Step 2는 앞 쪽의 기사를 보고 답을 맞춰 보세요.

정리하기 Choose a word from the box and complete the organizer.

> ○ questions ○ detect ○ carefully
> ○ nervous ○ mistakes ○ breathe

 **Main Idea** Lie detectors _________ lies by looking at what happens in the body.

 **Details**

1. They check the body when people answer ____________.

2. People may _________ faster and begin to sweat when they lie.

3. But lie detectors can make ____________.

Conclusion The machines are helpful, but we must use them ____________.

※ detect 감지하다   carefully 신중하게   mistake 실수

토론하기 Choose and circle the correct answers.

Do you agree with the **Conclusion** ?

※ even if 심지어 ~할 때도   truth 진실

A Fish That Eats Plastic!

A study says there are 170 trillion microplastics in the oceans. Although plastic pollution is getting worse, there's good news. Now, a robot fish can find them and clean them up. It swims like a real fish and eats plastic. This robot can carry 500 kilograms of waste. It is small and light but very strong. Scientists are testing it in oceans, rivers, and lakes. Many people are excited about this new technology.

Word Bank

microplastic 미세플라스틱

trillion 1조

although 비록 ~하지만

pollution 오염

carry 나르다

kilogram 킬로그램

waste 쓰레기

light 가벼운

be excited about ~에 대해 들뜨다, 신이 나다

technology 기술

⭐ 일부 로봇 물고기에는 빛을 이용해 미세플라스틱을 구별하는 센서가 들어 있다고 해요. 이 센서는 PET, 비닐, 폴리스티렌처럼 다양한 플라스틱 종류를 알아볼 수 있어서, 더 정밀하게 청소할 수 있다고 해요. 그래서 로봇이 그냥 '쓰레기'로 보는 게 아니라, 무엇인지 스스로 알아보고 골라낼 수 있는 거예요. 친구들이라면 이런 로봇에 어떤 기술을 더 넣어 보고 싶나요?

1 Fill in the blanks with the correct words from the box. One word will not be used.

> ○ robot　　○ microplastics　　○ carry　　○ light

1 There are many ________________ in the oceans.

2 The new ____________ fish can swim and clean up plastic in the ocean.

3 It may look small and ____________, but it is strong.

2 After reading the article, circle T(true) or F(false).

1 Plastic pollution in the oceans is getting worse.　　T　F

2 Scientists are testing the robot only in rivers.　　T　F

3 Complete the main idea sentence with words from the box.

> ○ swim　　○ remove　　○ air pollution　　○ environment

A robot fish can ________________ waste from the oceans and help the ________________.

✳ remove 없애다

 기사 쓰기 Unscramble the sentences below.

1 there are / a study says / in the oceans / 170 trillion microplastics

한 연구는 바다 안에 170조 개의 미세플라스틱이 있다고 말합니다.

2 plastic pollution / although / is getting worse, / good news / there's

비록 플라스틱 오염이 점점 더 심해지고 있지만, 좋은 소식이 있어요.

3 a robot fish / and clean them up / can find them / now,

이제는, 로봇 물고기가 그것들(미세플라스틱)을 찾아내고 치울 수 있어요.

4 and eats plastic / swims / like a real fish / it

그것은 진짜 물고기처럼 헤엄치고 플라스틱을 먹습니다.

5 can carry / this robot / of waste / 500 kilograms

이 로봇은 500킬로그램의 쓰레기를 나를 수 있습니다.

6 is small / but very strong / and light / it

그것은 작고 가볍지만 아주 튼튼해요.

7 in oceans, rivers, and lakes / are testing / scientists / it

과학자들은 그것을 바다, 강, 호수에서 시험하고 있어요.

8 are excited / many people / this new technology / about

많은 사람들은 이 새로운 기술에 대해 신이 나 있어요.

← Step 2는 앞 쪽의 기사를 보고 답을 맞춰 보세요.

- lakes
- technology
- worse
- fish-shaped
- collects
- strong

 **Main Idea** Now, _______________ robots can help clean the water.

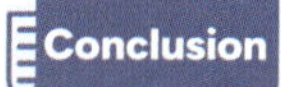 **Details**

1 Plastic pollution in the oceans is getting ___________.

2 This robot fish swims in the water and ___________ plastic.

3 Scientists are testing this robot in rivers and ___________, too.

Conclusion Many people are excited about this new _______________.

※ fish-shaped 물고기처럼 생긴   collect 모으다

Do you agree with the **Main Idea** ?

※ make a big difference 큰 영향을 주다

08

Word Bank

click
딸깍하는 소리를 내다

hurt 다친

stressed
스트레스를 받은

without ~ 없이

healthy 건강한

warn 경고하다

make changes
변화를 주다

stay safe
안전하게 있다

lead to 결과를 가져오다

farming 농사

Do Plants Talk?

In 2023, scientists found that plants make sounds. These clicking sounds happen when plants are hurt or stressed. People cannot hear the sounds without a special machine. The stressed plants clicked over 40 times in one hour. On the other hand, healthy plants made few or no sounds. Scientists think the sounds warn other plants. Other plants hear the sounds and make changes to stay safe. Plant sounds could lead to smarter farming in the future.

✪ 과학자들은 식물의 소리를 듣고, 언제 물을 줘야 할지 자동으로 알려주는 시스템을 개발 중이라고 해요. 이 기술이 발전하면, 식물이 "나 목말라요!"라고 신호를 보내는 순간 바로 물을 줄 수 있죠. 그러면 농부들은 물을 아끼면서도 식물을 더 똑똑하게 돌볼 수 있게 돼요. 이런 농장이 생기면, 농부들의 하루는 어떻게 달라질까요?

1 Fill in the blanks with the correct words from the box. One word will not be used.

> ○ machine   ○ safe   ○ warn   ○ healthy

1. Scientists used a special _____________ to hear the plant sounds.
2. There were few or no sounds from _____________ plants.
3. Other plants listen to the sounds and change to stay _____________.

2 After reading the article, circle T(true) or F(false).

1. Stressed plants clicked more than healthy plants.   T F
2. The clicking sounds were very loud.   T F

3 Complete the main idea sentence with words from the box.

> ○ farm   ○ pain   ○ mountain   ○ stress

A study found that plants make sounds when they are in _____________ or under _____________.

✳ in ~을 겪고 있는 상태에 있는   under ~을 받는 상태에 있는

1 scientists found that / in 2023, / plants / sounds / make

____

2023년에, 과학자들은 식물들이 소리를 낸다는 것을 발견했어요.

2 when / happen / are hurt or stressed / plants / these clicking sounds

____

이런 딸깍거리는 소리들은 식물이 다치거나 스트레스를 받을 때 일어납니다.

3 cannot hear / without / the sounds / a special machine / people

____

사람들은 특별한 기계 없이는 그 소리를 들을 수 없어요.

4 in one hour / clicked / over 40 times / the stressed plants

____

그 스트레스 받은 식물들은 한 시간 안에 40번 넘게 딸깍거렸어요.

5 few or no sounds / made / healthy plants / on the other hand,

____

반면에, 건강한 식물들은 거의 또는 전혀 소리를 내지 않았어요.

6 the sounds / scientists think / other plants / warn

____

과학자들은 그 소리들이 다른 식물들에게 경고한다고 생각합니다.

7 to stay safe / hear the sounds / other plants / and make changes

____

다른 식물들은 그 소리를 듣고 안전하게 있기 위해 변화를 줘요.

8 could lead to / plant sounds / in the future / smarter farming

____

식물이 내는 소리가 미래에는 더 스마트한 농업으로 이어질 수도 있어요.

← Step 2는 앞 쪽의 기사를 보고 답을 맞춰 보세요.

정리하기 **Choose a word from the box and complete the organizer.**

- without
- protect
- quiet
- feel
- farmers
- danger

Main Idea Plants make small sounds when they ___________ pain or stress.

Details

1 Stressed plants clicked a lot, but healthy plants stayed ________.

2 Scientists believe the sounds warn other plants of ___________.

3 When other plants hear the sounds, they make changes to ______________ themselves.

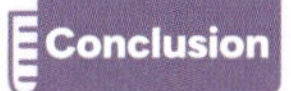
Conclusion In the future, these plant sounds could help _____________ grow plants better.

STEP 04

토론하기 **Choose and circle the correct answers.**

Do you agree with the  **Conclusion** ?

because plant sounds are not enough, so farmers still need to look carefully at their plants.

because farmers can use the sounds to know which plants need help.

Animals Need Quiet Homes, Too

Today, many animals live near people. However, loud noise from cars and machines can harm them. Some animals leave their homes because of noise. In the ocean, ship noise makes communicating hard for whales. One study says dolphins cannot communicate well in loud places. Loud sounds make animals scared or stressed. Some animals stop feeding their babies. It is time to think about how our noise affects animals.

Word Bank

quiet 조용한

noise 소음

harm 해를 주다

leave 떠나다

communicate 의사소통을 하다

dolphin 돌고래

scared 겁먹은

feed 먹이다

affect 영향을 주다

한 연구에 따르면, 도시의 소음 때문에 야생동물들이 밤에만 움직인다고 해요. 낮에는 사람과 소리가 많아서 무서워 숨는 일이 많다고 해요. 이런 변화는 동물들의 먹이 활동이나 쉬는 시간에도 영향을 줄 수 있어요. 도시에 사는 동물들을 위해 우리 친구들은 어떤 배려를 할 수 있을까요?

1 Fill in the blanks with the correct words from the box. One word will not be used.

> ○ quiet   ○ leave   ○ ship   ○ babies

1 Some animals ____________ their homes when it is too loud.

2 ____________ noise in the ocean makes it hard for whales to communicate.

3 Loud noise can stop animals from feeding their ____________.

2 After reading the article, circle T(true) or F(false).

1 Noises from ships helps dolphins communicate better.　　T　F

2 Loud sounds can make animals scared or stressed.　　T　F

3 Complete the main idea sentence with words from the box.

> ○ nature   ○ people   ○ well-being   ○ cars

Today, many animals live near ____________, but loud noise is a big problem for their ____________.

✳ well-being 건강과 행복, 웰빙

1 many animals / today, / near people / live

____

오늘날, 많은 동물들이 사람 가까이에서 살고 있어요.

2 loud noise / can harm them / from cars and machines / however,

____

하지만, 자동차와 기계에서 나는 시끄러운 소음이 그들(동물들)에게 해를 줄 수 있어요.

3 because of noise / leave / some animals / their homes

____

어떤 동물들은 소음 때문에 자기 집을 떠나기도 합니다.

4 ship noise / in the ocean, / for whales / makes communicating hard

____

바다에서는, 배에서 나는 소음이 고래들이 소통하는 것을 어렵게 만들어요.

5 dolphins / one study says / in loud places / cannot communicate well

____

한 연구는 돌고래들이 시끄러운 곳에서는 잘 소통할 수 없다고 말합니다.

6 make / scared or stressed / animals / loud sounds

____

시끄러운 소리는 동물들을 무섭게 하거나 스트레스를 받게 만들어요.

7 their babies / stop / some animals / feeding

____

어떤 동물들은 자기 새끼에게 먹이를 주는 것을 멈추기도 해요.

8 animals / to think about / it is time / affects / how our noise

____

우리의 소음이 동물들에게 어떤 영향을 주는지 생각해 봐야 할 때입니다.

← Step 2는 앞 쪽의 기사를 보고 답을 맞춰 보세요.

정리하기 Choose a word from the box and complete the organizer.

- stressed
- affects
- near
- communicating
- pollution
- feed

Main Idea Noise ______________ is harming animals.

Details

1. Many animals live __________ humans, but cars and machines make loud noises.

2. Some animals may feel ___________ and leave their homes.

3. Whales have a hard time ______________ because of noise from ships.

Conclusion We should care about how our noise ___________ animals.

※ noise pollution 소음 공해

토론하기 Choose and circle the correct answers.

Do you agree with the **Conclusion**?

Can Humans Make Diamonds?

Now, labs can make diamonds in just a few days. This is big news because it takes millions of years to grow them in nature. This makes lab-grown diamonds a lot cheaper. That's why they are also useful for many industries. For example, they can be used in things like special devices and space tools. Because of this, many companies are choosing lab diamonds today. In 2023, sales of lab diamonds grew by 20%. Lab diamonds are changing the future of science.

Word Bank

human 인간

lab 실험실

millions 수백만

nature 자연

lab-grown 실험실에서 만든

useful 유용한

industry 산업

device 장치

company 회사

sale 판매

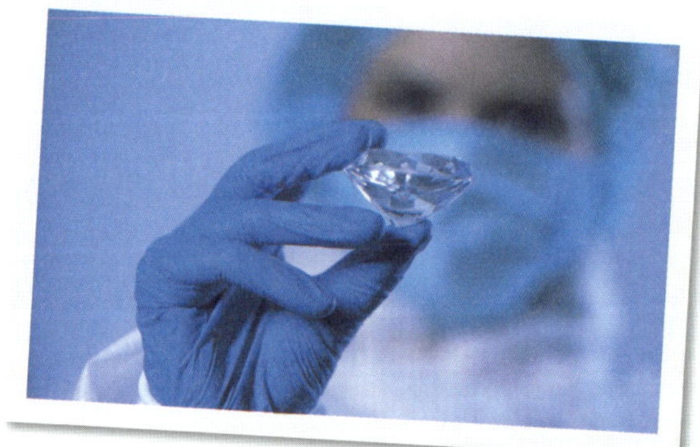

⭐ 다이아몬드는 몸속에 들어가는 센서나 인공 장기의 재료로 쓰이기도 해요. 실험실에서 만든 다이아몬드는 불순물이 적고 아주 깨끗해서, 몸속에서도 안정적으로 작동한다고 해요. 그래서 장기 이식 센서나 혈당 측정기, 뇌파 장비처럼 중요한 의료기기에 쓰이도록 개발 중이에요. 친구들이 미래 과학자나 발명가라면, 다이아몬드를 어디에 써 보고 싶나요?

1 Fill in the blanks with the correct words from the box. One word will not be used.

> ○ devices ○ news ○ nature ○ diamonds

1 Lab-grown _____________________ can be made in a few days.

2 They are cheaper than diamonds from _____________.

3 Many companies use them to make special _____________.

2 After reading the article, circle **T**(true) or **F**(false).

1 Lab-grown diamonds take millions of years to grow. T F

2 Sales of lab-grown diamonds went up in 2023. T F

3 Complete the main idea sentence with words from the box.

> ○ future ○ labs ○ industries ○ fake

Now, humans can grow diamonds in _____________, and these diamonds are useful for many _____________.

❋ fake 가짜의

1 labs / now, / can make / in just a few days / diamonds

이제는, 실험실은 다이아몬드를 단 며칠 만에 만들 수 있어요.

2 to grow them / millions of years / in nature / it takes / because

This is big news

이것은 자연에서는 그것들(다이아몬드들)이 생기는 데 수백만 년이 걸리기 때문에 큰 뉴스입니다.

3 a lot cheaper / makes / this / lab-grown diamonds

이것은 실험실에서 만든 다이아몬드를 훨씬 더 싸게 만들어요.

4 they / that's why / for many industries / are also useful

그렇기 때문에 그것들은 많은 산업에서 유용하기도 합니다.

5 and space tools / can be used / they / like special devices / in things

For example,

예를 들어, 그것들은 특별한 장치들과 우주 도구 같은 것들에 사용될 수 있어요.

6 are choosing / lab diamonds / many companies / because of this,

today.

이것 때문에, 오늘날 많은 회사들이 실험실 다이아몬드를 선택하고 있어요.

7 sales / in 2023, / grew / of lab diamonds / by 20%

2023년에는, 실험실 다이아몬드의 판매가 20% 증가하였습니다.

8 are changing / lab diamonds / of science / the future

실험실 다이아몬드는 과학의 미래를 바꾸고 있어요.

← Step 2는 앞 쪽의 기사를 보고 답을 맞춰 보세요.

- science
- expensive
- companies
- cheaper
- natural
- man-made

Main Idea Lab-grown diamonds, or ________________ diamonds, are made in just a few days.

Details

1 It takes millions of years to grow ______________ diamonds.

2 But lab-grown diamonds can be made quickly, so they're ______________.

3 So many ________ use them to make special devices and tools.

Conclusion These diamonds are helping the future of ___________.

※ natural 천연의 man-made 인공적인

Do you agree with the **Conclusion** ?

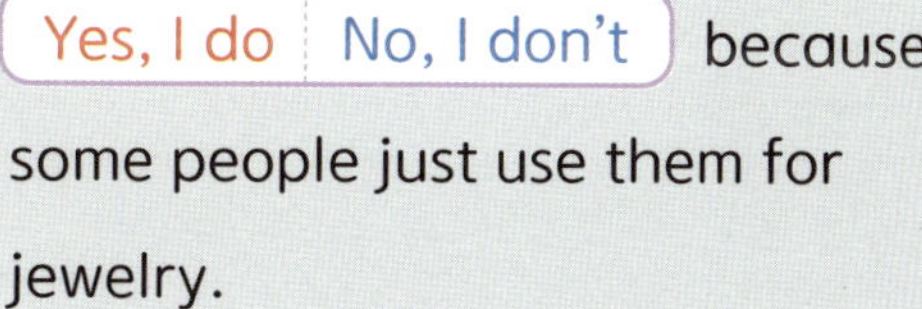

※ jewelry 보석류, 장신구

Food Waste Isn't Just about Food

A recent UN report says about 30% of food is wasted globally. However, wasting food is not just about food itself. Food takes land, water, and energy to grow. We lose all of that when food is wasted. That's not the only problem. Wasting food also puts harmful gases in the air. This happens because farms use machines, and moving food burns fuel. That's why wasting less food is important for the environment.

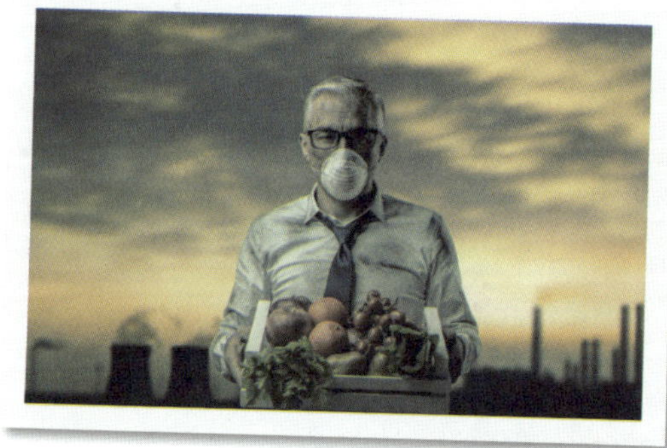

Word Bank

report 보고서

waste 낭비하다

globally 전 세계적으로

~ itself ~ 그 자체

energy 에너지

gas 가스

burn 연소시키다, 태우다

fuel 연료

environment 환경

세계자원연구소(WRI)에 따르면, 음식물 쓰레기를 절반으로 줄이면 2030년까지 온실가스를 크게 줄일 수 있다고 해요. 이건 자동차 4억 대가 줄어드는 것과 비슷한 효과예요. 그래서 여러 나라에서 음식물 쓰레기를 줄이는 캠페인을 많이 하고 있어요. 친구들은 음식을 남기지 않기 위해 어떤 습관을 가져 보고 싶나요?

1 Fill in the blanks with the correct words from the box. One word will not be used.

> ○ wasted   ○ grow   ○ energy   ○ burns

1 We need land and water to help food ____________.

2 When food is ____________, it harms the Earth.

3 Moving food ____________ fuel and produces bad gases.

2 After reading the article, circle **T**(true) or **F**(false).

1 Only a few countries have a food waste problem.   T   F

2 Wasting food means losing land, water, and energy, too.   T   F

3 Complete the main idea sentence with words from the box.

> ○ many   ○ throwing away   ○ cooking   ○ healthy

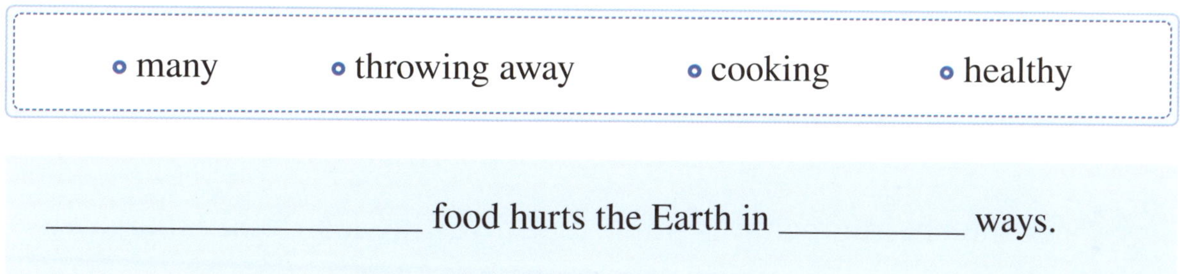

____________________ food hurts the Earth in __________ ways.

❈ throw away 버리다

1 says / a recent UN report / is wasted globally / about 30% of food

최근 UN 보고서는 전 세계적으로 음식의 약 30%가 낭비된다고 말해요.

2 wasting food / food itself / is not just about / however,

하지만, 음식을 낭비하는 것은 단지 음식 그 자체에 대한 것만은 아니에요.

3 to grow / takes / food / land, water, and energy

음식은 자라기 위해 땅, 물, 그리고 에너지를 필요로 해요.

4 lose / we / all of that / food is wasted / when

음식이 버려질 때 우리는 그것들을 모두 잃게 돼요.

5 problem / that's not / the only

그것이 유일한 문제는 아니에요.

6 also puts / wasting food / in the air / harmful gases

음식을 버리는 건 공기 속에 해로운 가스를 만들기도 해요.

7 use machines, / burns fuel / and moving food / farms / this happens because

이것은 농장들이 기계를 사용하고, 음식을 옮기는 것은 연료를 태우기 때문에 일어나요.

8 for the environment / is important / wasting less food / that's why

그렇기 때문에 음식을 덜 낭비하는 것이 환경을 위해 중요하답니다.

← Step 2는 앞 쪽의 기사를 보고 답을 맞춰 보세요.

- impact
- gases
- resources
- food
- globally
- waste

Main Idea Wasting food has a bigger ____________ on the environment than we think.

Details

1 Wasting food uses ____________ like land, water, and energy.

2 So if we waste ____________, we also waste the things used to make it.

3 Machines and fuel also add harmful ____________ to the air.

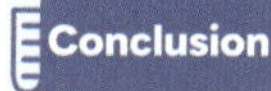
Conclusion It is important to ____________ less food to help our planet.

✳ impact 영향 resource 자원

STEP
04 토론하기 Choose and circle the correct answers.

Do you agree with the **Main Idea**?

Word Bank

fake 가짜의

protection 보호

COVID-19 코로나19

vaccine 백신

work 작용하다, 작동하다

immune system 면역 체계

germ 병균

without ~ 없이

remember 기억하다

Fake Germs, Real Protection

Since COVID-19, more people want to know how vaccines work. Our bodies have an immune system that fights germs.

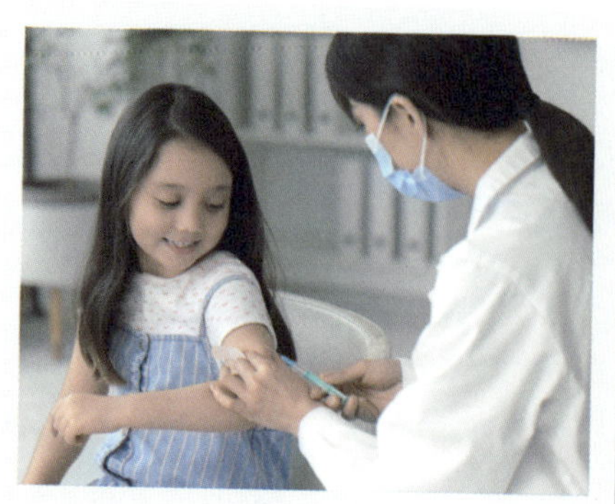

Vaccines help this system learn to fight germs. They use weak or fake germs to do this. This helps the body learn without getting sick. After that, the immune system remembers the germs. As a result, the body fights them faster and better next time. That's why getting vaccines is a smart way to protect your body.

코로나19 백신에는 mRNA라는 새로운 기술이 쓰였어요. 이 기술 덕분에 예전 백신보다 훨씬 더 빠르고 쉽게 만들 수 있었다고 해요. 앞으로 이 기술로 암이나 다른 병도 예방할 수 있을지 연구 중이라고 하네요. 친구들은 백신 기술이 더 발전하면 어떤 병을 막을 수 있을지 생각해 본 적 있나요?

1 Fill in the blanks with the correct words from the box. One word will not be used.

> ○ weak   ○ germs   ○ immune   ○ better

(1) The _______________ system protects our bodies from germs.

(2) Vaccines help our bodies practice fighting ___________.

(3) Vaccines use ___________ or fake germs.

2 After reading the article, circle T(true) or F(false).

(1) Since the COVID-19 pandemic, more people want to understand vaccines.　　T　F

(2) After getting a vaccine, the immune system forgets the germs.　　T　F

※ pandemic 전 세계적인 질병

3 Complete the main idea sentence with words from the box.

> ○ vaccines   ○ protection   ○ doctor   ○ sickness

_______________ let the immune system get ready before a real _______________ comes.

※ sickness 질병

1 more people / since COVID-19, / how vaccines work / want to know

코로나19 이후로, 더 많은 사람들이 백신이 어떻게 작용하는지 알고 싶어 해요.

2 have / that fights germs / an immune system / our bodies

우리 몸은 병균과 싸우는 면역 체계를 가지고 있어요.

3 germs / learn to fight / help / vaccines / this system

백신은 이 체계가 병균과 싸우는 법을 배우도록 도와줘요.

4 use / they / to do this / weak or fake germs

그것들은 이것을 하기 위해 약하거나 가짜 병균을 사용해요.

5 helps / without getting sick / the body learn / this

이것은 몸이 아프지 않고 배우도록 도와줘요.

6 the germs / the immune system / after that, / remembers

그 다음에, 면역 체계는 그 병균들을 기억해요.

7 the body / As a result, / faster and better / fights them / next time

결과적으로, 몸이 다음번에 그것들(병균들)과 더 빠르고 더 잘 싸워요.

8 getting vaccines / that's why / to protect your body / is a smart way

그렇기 때문에 백신을 맞는 것이 몸을 지키는 똑똑한 방법이랍니다.

← Step 2는 앞 쪽의 기사를 보고 답을 맞춰 보세요.

03 정리하기 Choose a word from the box and complete the organizer.

- protect
- weak
- remembers
- safe
- faster
- cough

Main Idea Vaccines help the body learn about germs in a __________ way.

Details
1 They use __________ germs to train the immune system.
2 Then, the immune system __________ the germs.
3 After that, the body can fight real germs __________ and better.

Conclusion So vaccines are a smart choice to __________ the body.

✳ train 훈련시키다

04 토론하기 Choose and circle the correct answers.

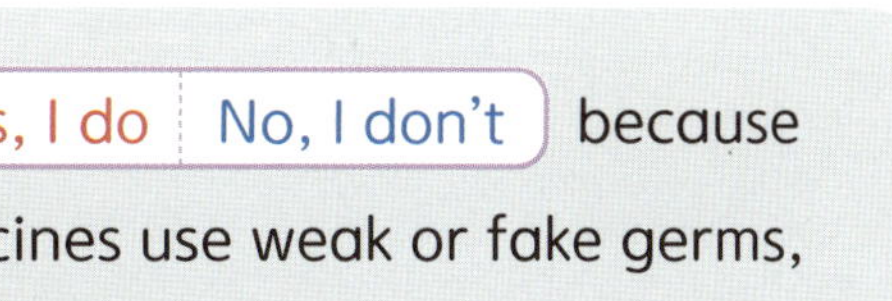

Word Bank

save (water / **the world**) (물을) 아끼다 / (세상을) 구하다

climate change 기후 변화

drought 가뭄

global 전 세계적인

affect 영향을 미치다

turn off 끄다, 잠그다

while ~하는 동안

bowl 그릇, 대야

rinse 헹구다

vegetable 채소

action 행동

Save Water, Save the World!

Water is becoming harder to find in many places. This is happening because of climate change and droughts. A global study found that 1 in 3 people don't have clean water. This problem affects both rich and poor countries. That's why everyone should help. At home, we can turn off the water while brushing our teeth. Using a bowl to rinse fruits and vegetables helps, too. Small actions like these can save a lot of water.

세계보건기구에 따르면, 매년 약 200만 명이 더러운 물 때문에 병에 걸려 목숨을 잃는다고 해요. 깨끗한 물이 없는 지역에서는 손 씻기나 요리도 어렵다고 해요. 그래서 깨끗한 물을 아끼고 지키는 일이 정말 중요해요. 친구들은 물을 아끼기 위해 어떤 습관을 가져 보고 싶나요?

1 Fill in the blanks with the correct words from the box. One word will not be used.

> ○ droughts   ○ save   ○ rinse   ○ water

1 It's getting difficult to find ___________ in many areas.

2 This happens because of climate change and _____________.

3 We can ___________ water at home with small actions.

2 After reading the article, circle T(true) or F(false).

1 It is hard to find clean water only in poor countries.   T   F

2 A study says 1 in 3 people can't find clean water.   T   F

3 Complete the main idea sentence with words from the box.

> ○ wisely   ○ flood   ○ climate change   ○ carelessly

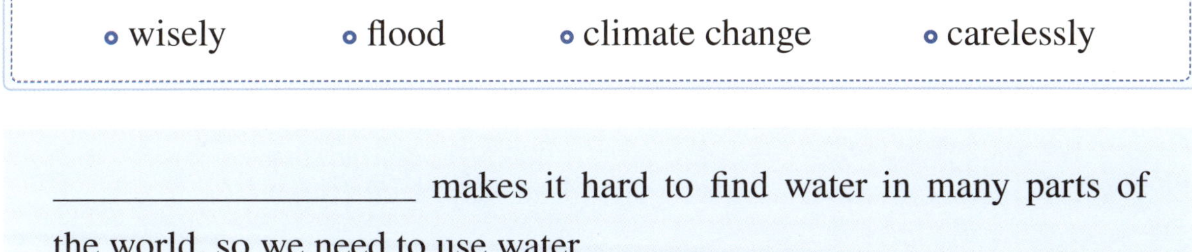

___________________ makes it hard to find water in many parts of the world, so we need to use water ___________.

※ flood 홍수   carelessly 부주의하게

기사 쓰기 Unscramble the sentences below.

1 is becoming / in many places / harder to find / water

물은 많은 곳에서 찾기 더 어려워지고 있어요.

2 and droughts / because of / this is happening / climate change

이것은 기후 변화와 가뭄 때문에 발생하고 있어요.

3 found that / a global study / 1 in 3 people / clean water / don't have

세계적인 연구는 3명 중 1명이 깨끗한 물을 가지고 있지 않다는 것을 발견했어요.

4 affects / this problem / rich and poor countries / both

이 문제는 부유한 나라와 가난한 나라 둘 다에 영향을 줘요.

5 everyone / that's why / help / should

그렇기 때문에 모두가 도와야 해요.

6 can turn off the water / we / brushing our teeth / while / at home,

집에서, 우리는 이를 닦는 동안 물을 잠글 수 있어요.

7 helps, too / to rinse / using a bowl / fruits and vegetables

과일과 채소를 씻을 때 대야를 사용하는 것도 도움이 돼요.

8 a lot of / can save / water / small actions like these

이런 것들과 같은 작은 행동들이 많은 물을 아낄 수 있어요.

← Step 2는 앞 쪽의 기사를 보고 답을 맞춰 보세요.

정리하기 Choose a word from the box and complete the organizer.

> - simple   - affects   - find
> - vegetables   - off   - dry

Main Idea Clean water is hard to __________ in many parts of the world.

Details

1 This is happening because of climate change and __________ weather.

2 This problem __________ many countries, both rich and poor.

3 Turning __________ water when brushing our teeth or using a bowl to rinse fruits can help save water.

Conclusion These actions are __________ but can save a lot of water.

토론하기 Choose and circle the correct answers.

Do you agree with the **Conclusion** ?

※ cause 원인

Can Robots Feel Emotions?

Word Bank

emotion 감정

even 심지어

respond
반응하다, 응답하다

be surprised 놀라다

truly 정말로

data 데이터

collect
수집하다, 모으다

response 반응

be based on
~에 기반하다

code 코드
(프로그램 명령)

Today, robots can show emotions like humans. They smile, talk kindly, and even respond to people's faces. Many people are surprised because these actions look real. In 2023, a study found that 65% of people think robots understand feelings. But robots do not truly feel emotions like humans. They only copy feelings by using data that they collect. Their responses are based on code, not real emotions. Still, this helps them work better with people.

⭐ 일부 로봇은 사람의 목소리 톤까지 분석해서 기분이 좋은지, 화가 났는지 알아낸다고 해요. 그래서 말을 걸 때 더 친절하게 반응할 수 있다고 해요. 이런 기술은 주로 서비스 로봇이나 상담 로봇에 사용되고 있어요. 친구들은 이런 로봇이 또 어떤 분야에서 도움이 될 수 있을지 생각해 본 적 있나요?

1 Fill in the blanks with the correct words from the box. One word will not be used.

> ∘ faces   ∘ robots   ∘ humans   ∘ real

(1) ______________ can smile and talk like people.

(2) They can also respond to people's ______________.

(3) These actions look ______________, so many people are surprised.

2 After reading the article, circle **T**(true) or **F**(false).

(1) A 2023 study says many people think robots understand feelings.   T   F

(2) Robots use collected data to copy people's feelings.   T   F

3 Complete the main idea sentence with words from the box.

> ∘ emotions   ∘ speak   ∘ code   ∘ understand

Robots can show ______________ like humans, but they don't truly ______________ feelings.

1 robots / today, / emotions like humans / can show

오늘날, 로봇들은 사람처럼 감정을 보여줄 수 있어요.

2 to people's faces / smile, talk kindly, / they / and even respond

그것들은 웃고, 친절하게 말하고, 심지어 사람의 얼굴에 반응하기도 해요.

3 are surprised / many people / because / look real / these actions

이런 행동들이 진짜처럼 보이기 때문에 많은 사람들이 놀라요.

4 robots understand feelings / 65% of people think / a study found that

In 2023,

2023년에, 한 연구는 사람들의 65%는 로봇이 감정을 이해한다고 생각한다는 것을 발견했어요.

5 do not truly feel / but / robots / like humans / emotions

하지만 로봇은 사람처럼 정말로 감정을 느끼지는 않아요.

6 only copy / they / feelings / that they collect / by using data

그것들은 단지 자신들이 수집하는 데이터를 사용해서 감정을 흉내 낼 뿐이에요.

7 are based on / their responses / code, / not real emotions

그것들의 반응은 코드에 기반할 것이지, 진짜 감정이 아니에요.

8 helps them / this / with people / work better / still,

그래도, 이것은 그것들이 사람들과 더 잘 일하도록 도와줘요.

← Step 2는 앞 쪽의 기사를 보고 답을 맞춰 보세요.

정리하기 **Choose a word from the box and complete the organizer.**

- feelings
- human-like
- collect
- work
- respond
- code

Main Idea Robots show _______________ emotions, but they don't really feel these emotions.

Details

1. They can talk with a kind voice and _______ to people's faces.
2. Some people think robots understand _________ like humans do.
3. But they only copy feelings by using _________ and data.

Conclusion Still, this helps them ___________ well with people.

※ human-like 사람 같은

토론하기 **Choose and circle the correct answers.**

※ the elderly 노인들, 어르신들

Too Many Clothes, Too Much Waste

Fast fashion is a growing problem around the world. It means people buy lots of cheap clothes. They wear these clothes only a few times. After that, they throw the clothes away. Each year, over 92 million tons of clothes are wasted. This creates more pollution and harms the planet. To help, we can wear clothes longer or buy eco-friendly clothes. How we choose and use clothes can help the planet.

Word Bank

fast fashion
패스트 패션
(빠른 유행의 옷)

cheap 값싼

throw away
버리다

million 백만

ton 톤(무게 단위)
(1ton = 1,000kg)

pollution 오염

eco-friendly
친환경적인

choose 선택하다

한국환경공단에 따르면, 우리나라에서 매년 약 12만 톤의 헌옷이 분리배출된다고 해요. 게다가 일반 쓰레기와 함께 버려지는 옷까지 합치면 수십만 톤에 이른다고 해요. 이렇게 많은 옷이 버려지면서 환경에 큰 부담이 되고 있어요. 이런 낭비를 줄이기 위해 우리는 어떤 노력을 할 수 있을까요?

1 Fill in the blanks with the correct words from the box. One word will not be used.

> ○ eco-friendly   ○ cheap   ○ longer   ○ problem

1 Fast fashion is a ______________ in many parts of the world.

2 People buy more clothes because they are ______________.

3 Wearing clothes ______________ can help the planet.

2 After reading the article, circle T(true) or F(false).

1 People waste over 92 million tons of clothes every year.　　T　F

2 Fast fashion lets people wear clothes for many years.　　T　F

3 Complete the main idea sentence with words from the box.

> ○ shopping   ○ fast fashion   ○ pollution   ○ clothes

______________________ is hurting the planet because it creates a lot of waste and ______________.

1 is / fast fashion / around the world / a growing problem

____

전 세계적으로 패스트 패션은 점점 커지는 문제예요.

2 lots of cheap clothes / people / it means / buy

____

그것은 사람들이 값싼 옷을 많이 산다는 뜻이에요.

3 wear / only a few times / these clothes / they

____

그들(사람들)은 이 옷들을 몇 번만 입고 말아요.

4 throw the clothes away / they / after that,

____

그 다음에, 그들(사람들)은 그 옷들을 버려요.

5 over 92 million tons / each year, / are wasted / of clothes

____

매년, 9천 2백만 톤이 넘는 옷이 낭비됩니다.

6 creates / and harms the planet / more pollution / this

____

이것은 더 많은 오염을 만들고 지구를 해쳐요.

7 eco-friendly clothes / can wear clothes / or buy / longer / we

To help,
____

도움이 되기 위해, 우리는 옷을 더 오래 입거나 친환경 옷을 살 수 있어요.

8 choose and use clothes / how we / the planet / can help

____

우리가 옷을 고르고 사용하는 방식이 지구를 도울 수 있어요.

← Step 2는 앞 쪽의 기사를 보고 답을 맞춰 보세요.

정리하기 Choose a word from the box and complete the organizer.

- harms
- throwing
- how
- serious
- many
- eco-friendly

Main Idea Fast fashion is a ___________ problem around the world.

Details

1. People wear cheap clothes only a few times before _________ them away.

2. This creates more pollution and ___________ the Earth.

3. We can help by using clothes longer and by buying _________ clothes.

Conclusion ___________ we buy and wear clothes can help the environment.

※ serious 심각한

STEP 04

토론하기 Choose and circle the correct answers.

Do you agree with the **Conclusion**?

Word Bank

self-driving car
자율주행차

sensor 센서

AI 인공지능

goal 목표

safely 안전하게

accident 사고

system error
시스템 오류

wonder 궁금해하다

situation 상황

clear 명확한, 분명한

No Driver, No Problem?

Peoplc around the world are excited about self-driving cars. Self-driving cars can move without drivers. They

use cameras, sensors, and AI to drive. In 2024, over 25 cities tested this new technology. The goal is to help people travel more safely in the future. But some people worry about accidents and system errors. Others wonder what the cars will do in difficult situations. We need clear rules and more testing for the future.

⭐ 2024년 한국 국토교통부는 세종시에서 자율주행차의 실제 도로 운행을 더 확대할 거라고 발표했어요. 세종시는 스마트시티로 개발 중이라 새로운 기술을 시험하기에 가장 적합한 도시라고 해요. 이런 실험은 자율주행차가 우리 일상에 자리잡기 위한 중요한 걸음이 될 수 있어요. 친구들은 자율주행차가 생기면 우리의 하루가 어떻게 달라질 거라고 생각하나요?

1 Fill in the blanks with the correct words from the box. One word will not be used.

> ○ drivers   ○ safer   ○ cameras   ○ tested

(1) Self-driving cars do not need ___________.

(2) Some cities ___________ this new technology in 2024.

(3) They hope these cars will make traveling ___________ in the future.

2 After reading the article, circle T(true) or F(false).

(1) Self-driving cars use cameras, sensors, and AI to drive. T F

(2) Everyone feels happy about using self-driving cars. T F

3 Complete the main idea sentence with words from the box.

> ○ rules   ○ errors   ○ technology   ○ speed

Self-driving cars are an exciting _______________, but they need more testing and clear ___________.

1 self-driving cars / are excited / people around the world / about

전 세계 사람들이 자율주행차에 들떠 있어요.

2 can move / drivers / without / self-driving cars

자율주행차는 운전자 없이 움직일 수 있어요.

3 cameras, sensors, and AI / use / to drive / they

그것들은 운전하기 위해서 카메라, 센서, 그리고 인공지능을 사용해요.

4 over 25 cities / in 2024, / this new technology / tested

2024년에는, 25개가 넘는 도시들이 이 새로운 기술을 시험했어요.

5 in the future / is to help people / the goal / travel more safely

그 목적은 사람들이 미래에 더 안전하게 이동하도록 돕는 것이에요.

6 some people / but / accidents and system errors / worry about

하지만 어떤 사람들은 사고와 시스템 오류에 대해 걱정해요.

7 what the cars / in difficult situations / will do / others wonder

다른 사람들은 차가 어려운 상황에서 무엇을 할지 궁금해해요.

8 need / we / for the future / clear rules and more testing

미래를 위해 명확한 규칙과 더 많은 시험이 필요합니다.

← Step 2는 앞 쪽의 기사를 보고 답을 맞춰 보세요.

- testing
- accidents
- travel
- without
- situations
- concern

Main Idea People show both excitement and ___________ about self-driving cars.

Details
1 Self-driving cars can move ___________ drivers inside.
2 They may help many people ___________ safely in the future.
3 But some people worry about ___________ and system errors.

Conclusion We need clear rules and more ___________ before people can use them.

✳ concern 걱정, 우려

STEP
04 토론하기 Choose and circle the correct answers.

✳ reduce 줄이다   hacker (컴퓨터 시스템에 침입하여 조작하는) 해커

The Earth Is Warming Too Fast

The planet is warming faster than ever. Global temperatures go up by 0.2°C every 10 years. That number seems small, but it is dangerous for life. Floods, droughts, and fires may get worse. Some plants and animals may disappear forever. Scientists also warn that if the Earth gets 1.5°C hotter, things will get much worse. This means very big and dangerous climate problems. We need to help save our planet before it's too late.

Word Bank

warm 따뜻해지다

than ever 그 어느 때보다도

global temperature 지구 평균 기온

seem ~처럼 보이다

dangerous 위험한

flood 홍수

disappear 사라지다

things 상황

climate 기후

before it's too late 너무 늦기 전에

⭐ 지구 온도가 1.5도 오르면, 농작물 재배에 필요한 비와 기온이 달라져서 식량 생산이 줄 수 있어요. 특히 쌀, 밀, 옥수수 같은 주요 곡물 생산량이 줄어들면, 전 세계 사람들이 먹을 것이 부족해질 수 있다고 해요. 유엔식량농업기구(FAO)는 2050년까지 기후 변화로 인해 식량 위기가 더 자주 올 수 있다고 해요. 이런 일이 일어나지 않도록, 친구들은 어떤 노력을 해 볼 수 있을까요?

1 Fill in the blanks with the correct words from the box. One word will not be used.

> ○ temperature   ○ forever   ○ warming   ○ floods

1 The Earth is _____________ too fast.

2 Big problems like droughts and ___________ may happen more often.

3 We may lose some plants and animals ___________.

2 After reading the article, circle T(true) or F(false).

1 The planet is getting colder over time.   T F

2 Problems will get much worse if the Earth gets 1.5°C hotter.   T F

3 Complete the main idea sentence with words from the box.

> ○ slower   ○ faster   ○ before   ○ the Sun

Our planet is getting warmer ___________ than ___________.

1 is warming / the planet / than ever / faster

____

우리 행성(지구)은 그 어느 때보다 더 빠르게 따뜻해지고 있어요.

2 go up / every 10 years / by 0.2°C / global temperatures

____

지구 평균 기온은 10년마다 0.2도씩 올라가요.

3 dangerous for life / seems small, / that number / but it is

____

그 숫자는 작아 보이지만, 생명체에게는 위험해요.

4 may get / floods, droughts, and fires / worse

____

홍수, 가뭄, 그리고 산불이 더 심해질 수도 있어요.

5 may disappear / some plants and animals / forever

____

어떤 식물들과 동물들은 영원히 사라질 수도 있어요.

6 gets 1.5°C hotter, / will get much worse / things / if the Earth

Scientists also warn that
____

과학자들은 또한 지구가 1.5도 더 뜨거워지면, 상황은 훨씬 더 나빠질 것이라고 경고해요.

7 this means / climate problems / very big and dangerous

____

이것은 매우 크고 위험한 기후 문제들을 의미합니다.

8 before it's too late / need to help / we / save our planet

____

너무 늦기 전에 우리는 우리 지구를 구하는 것을 도와야 합니다.

← Step 2는 앞 쪽의 기사를 보고 답을 맞춰 보세요.

정리하기 Choose a word from the box and complete the organizer.

- fires
- disappear
- protect
- quickly
- decade
- hotter

Main Idea The Earth is getting warmer more ______________ than ever.

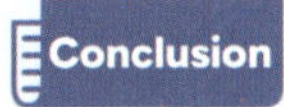

Details

1 Global temperatures rise by 0.2°C every ______________.

2 ______________, droughts, and floods can get worse.

3 Some plants and animals may ______________ and never come back.

Conclusion We must ______________ the planet before it's too late.

❋ decade 10년

토론하기 Choose and circle the correct answers.

Do you agree with the **Conclusion** ?

Smarter Arms and Legs

Word Bank

bionic 생체공학의

act (like)
(~처럼) 행동하다, 작동하다

signal 신호

sensor 센서

prevent
막다, 예방하다

fall 넘어지다

chance 가능성

bring hope
희망을 주다

Bionic arms and legs are getting smarter. They are machine parts that act like real arms and legs. For example, some bionic arms can read signals from the brain. They let people move their arms just by thinking. Bionic legs are also getting better. They have smart sensors to help prevent people from falling. A study says they can help lower the chances of falling by about 45%. These new changes are bringing hope to many people.

⭐ 요즘은 손가락 하나하나까지 움직일 수 있는 바이오닉 손도 있다고 해요. 게다가 어떤 바이오닉 손(사람 손처럼 움직이는 기계 의수)은 물건을 만졌을 때의 촉감까지 느낄 수 있다고 해요. 이건 손에 닿는 압력을 전기로 바꾸는 센서 덕분이에요. 친구들은 감각이 느껴지는 손이 없던 사람에게 그 손이 생긴다면, 그 사람의 하루가 어떻게 달라질지 상상해 본 적 있나요?

1　Fill in the blanks with the correct words from the box. One word will not be used.

> ○ machine　　○ thinking　　○ real　　○ act

(1) Bionic arms and legs are smart ______________ parts.

(2) They move like ____________ arms and legs.

(3) Some bionic arms move just by ______________.

2　After reading the article, circle T(true) or F(false).

(1) Bionic arms are getting worse and harder to use.　　　T　F

(2) Smart sensors in bionic legs help lower the chances of people falling.　　　T　F

3　Complete the main idea sentence with words from the box.

> ○ smarter　　○ human　　○ bionic　　○ faster

______________ arms and legs are getting ______________.

1 smarter / are getting / bionic arms and legs

바이오닉 팔과 다리는 점점 더 똑똑해지고 있어요.

2 machine parts / are / real arms and legs / that act like / they

그것들은 진짜 팔과 다리처럼 행동하는 기계 부품이에요.

3 from the brain / can read / some bionic arms / signals / for example,

예를 들어, 어떤 바이오닉 팔은 뇌에서 오는 신호를 읽을 수 있어요.

4 let people / just by thinking / move their arms / they

이것들은 사람들이 생각하는 것만으로도 그들의 팔을 움직일 수 있게 해 줘요.

5 better / are also getting / bionic legs

바이오닉 다리도 점점 더 발전하고 있어요.

6 have / they / to help prevent / smart sensors / people from falling

그것들은 사람들이 넘어지는 것을 막도록 도와주는 스마트 센서를 가지고 있습니다.

7 can help lower / they / of falling by about 45% / the chances

A study says

한 연구는 그것들은 넘어질 가능성을 약 45% 낮추는 데 도움을 줄 수 있다고 말합니다.

8 to many people / are bringing / these new changes / hope

이러한 새로운 변화들은 많은 사람들에게 희망을 주고 있어요.

← Step 2는 앞 쪽의 기사를 보고 답을 맞춰 보세요.

정리하기 Choose a word from the box and complete the organizer.

- control
- less
- limbs
- more
- hope
- signals

Main Idea Bionic ___________ are getting smarter.

Details

1. Some bionic arms can move by reading ___________ from the brain.

2. They help people ___________ their arms by thinking.

3. Smart sensors in bionic legs help people fall ________ often.

Conclusion These smart tools give people new ___________.

※ control 조종하다, 제어하다 limbs 사지(팔, 다리)

토론하기 Choose and circle the correct answers.

Do you agree with the **Conclusion**?

Fun Festivals, Big Trash

Festivals bring music, food, and fun. But they also create a lot of waste. One festival in Seoul created 50 tons of trash in 2022. That's as heavy as 40 cars! Because of this, eco-friendly events are getting more attention. For example, these events use fewer plastic items. Some events ask visitors to bring their own cups. It's a small but important step to help the environment.

Word Bank

festival 축제

trash 쓰레기

ton 톤(무게 단위)

eco-friendly 친환경적인

attention 관심

visitor 방문객

own 자기 자신의

environment 환경

⭐ 행사에서 생기는 쓰레기의 대부분은 일회용 컵, 포크, 비닐봉지라고 해요. 이런 플라스틱은 땅에서 썩는 데 100년 이상 걸려요. 그래서 요즘은 아예 일회용품을 안 쓰는 축제들도 생기고 있어요. 친구들은 축제에 갈 때 어떤 물건을 챙겨가면 좋을지 생각해 본 적 있나요?

1 Fill in the blanks with the correct words from the box. One word will not be used.

> • festivals   • plastic   • waste   • own

(1) People enjoy the music, food, and fun at ____________.

(2) But festivals also make a lot of ____________.

(3) Some eco-friendly events try to use less ____________.

2 After reading the article, circle T(true) or F(false).

(1) A festival in Seoul created trash as heavy as 40 cars.　T　F

(2) Some people bring their own cups to eco-friendly events.　T　F

3 Complete the main idea sentence with words from the box.

> • eco-friendly   • toxic   • trash   • music

People throw away a lot of ___________ at festivals, so many people want to make them more ________________.

❋ toxic 유해한

1 music, food, and fun / festivals / bring

____

축제들은 음악, 음식, 그리고 즐거움을 가져와요.

2 also create / they / a lot of waste / but

____

하지만 그것들은 많은 쓰레기도 만들어 내요.

3 created / one festival in Seoul / in 2022 / 50 tons of trash

____

2022년에 서울의 한 축제는 50톤의 쓰레기를 만들었어요.

4 40 cars! / as heavy as / that's

____

그것은 자동차 40대만큼 무거워요!

5 eco-friendly events / more attention / are getting / because of this,

____

이것 때문에, 친환경적인 행사들이 더 많은 관심을 받고 있어요.

6 use / these events / fewer plastic items / for example,

____

예를 들어, 이런 행사들은 플라스틱 물건을 더 적게 사용해요.

7 ask / some events / their own cups / visitors to bring

____

어떤 행사들은 방문객들에게 그들 자신의 컵을 가져오라고 요청해요.

8 the environment / a small but important step / it's / to help

____

이것은 환경을 돕기 위한 작지만 중요한 걸음입니다.

← Step 2는 앞 쪽의 기사를 보고 답을 맞춰 보세요.

- visitors
- create
- fewer
- important
- recycle
- festival

 **Main Idea** Festivals can be fun but ______________ a lot of waste.

 **Details**

1 One ______________ in Seoul made 50 tons of trash.

2 Eco-friendly events use ______________ plastic items.

3 Some ask ______________ to bring their own cups.

Conclusion This is a small but ______________ step to help the environment.

※ recycle 재활용하다

STEP 04 토론하기 Choose and circle the correct answers.

Do you agree with the **Detail 3** ?

Is Nuclear Power Worth the Risk?

Many people want clean energy to save the Earth. Nuclear power makes a lot of energy without creating carbon gas. One nuclear plant can give power to about 1 million homes. But accidents like the one at Fukushima worry people. Nuclear waste also stays dangerous for thousands of years. Some think it is not worth the risk. Others say we need it for clean energy. The debate continues as we fight climate change.

✿ 2011년, 일본 후쿠시마에서 큰 지진과 쓰나미로 원자력 발전소가 폭발하는 사고가 발생했어요. 이 사고로 방사능이 퍼지면서 많은 사람이 대피했고, 지금도 그 지역에는 사람이 살지 못해요. 이 일로 원자력 발전이 안전한지에 대한 걱정이 많아졌어요. 친구들은 지구를 위해 원자력 발전소를 계속 이용해야 한다고 생각하나요, 아니면 멈춰야 한다고 생각하나요?

1 Fill in the blanks with the correct words from the box. One word will not be used.

> ○ carbon   ○ continue   ○ waste   ○ nuclear

(1) ____________ power is a type of clean energy.

(2) It does not make ____________ gas.

(3) Nuclear ____________ is dangerous for years.

2 After reading the article, circle T(true) or F(false).

(1) One nuclear plant can power 1 million homes.　　T　F

(2) All people agree that nuclear power is safe.　　T　F

※ power 전기를 공급하다

3 Complete the main idea sentence with words from the box.

> ○ risks   ○ electricity   ○ dangerous   ○ clean

People want ____________ energy, but nuclear power comes with some ____________ .

※ electricity 전기

1 want / to save the Earth / clean energy / many people

____

많은 사람들은 지구를 구하기 위해 깨끗한 에너지를 원해요.

2 makes / nuclear power / without creating carbon gas / a lot of energy

____

원자력은 탄소가스를 만들지 않고 많은 에너지를 만들어요.

3 to about 1 million homes / can give / one nuclear plant / power

____

하나의 원자력 발전소는 약 백만 가구에 전력을 줄 수 있습니다.

4 accidents / but / worry people / like the one at Fukushima

____

하지만 후쿠시마에서 있었던 것과 같은 사고는 사람들을 걱정하게 해요.

5 also stays / nuclear waste / for thousands of years / dangerous

____

원자력 폐기물은 또한 수천 년 동안 위험한 상태로 남아 있습니다.

6 it / the risk / is not worth / some think

____

어떤 사람들은 그것이 위험을 감당할 만한 가치가 없다고 생각해요.

7 we / need it / for clean energy / others say

____

다른 사람들은 우리가 깨끗한 에너지를 위해 그것이 필요하다고 말해요.

8 continues / the debate / climate change / as we fight

____

우리가 기후 변화와 싸우는 동안 그 논쟁은 계속돼요.

← Step 2는 앞 쪽의 기사를 보고 답을 맞춰 보세요.

정리하기 Choose a word from the box and complete the organizer.

- low
- energy
- accidents
- climate change
- clean
- high

Main Idea Nuclear power gives us a lot of _____________ without creating carbon gas.

Details

1. But _____________ and nuclear waste worry many people.
2. Some people think the risks are too __________.
3. Others say we need it to make __________ energy.

Conclusion The debate continues as we try to fix _____________________.

토론하기 Choose and circle the correct answers.

Do you agree with the **Main Idea** ?

✳ solar 태양의

Word Bank

bottled water
플라스틱 병에 든 물(생수)

waste
낭비하다, 쓰레기

even worse
더 나쁜 것은

microplastic
미세 플라스틱

expert 전문가

tap water 수돗물

in addition 게다가

tumbler
텀블러(재사용 컵)

instead 대신에

reduce 줄이다

The Truth about Bottled Water

Many people around the world drink bottled water. But making bottles wastes a lot of oil, water, and energy. Even worse, the water inside the bottles may not be safe. In 2021, a study found that 93% of bottled water has microplastics. Because of this, some experts say tap water is a safer choice. In addition, many people use these bottles once and then throw them away. So using a tumbler instead can help reduce waste. Small changes like these help both our health and the Earth.

⭐ 최근 연구에 따르면 생수 1리터에 평균 24만 개의 나노플라스틱이 들어 있다고 해요. 이런 작은 입자는 혈류를 따라 몸속 깊은 장기까지 갈 수 있어요. 그래서 일부 전문가들은 수돗물이 더 안전한 선택일 수 있다고 말해요. 친구들은 우리 몸과 지구를 위해 어떤 물을 고르는 게 좋을지 생각해 본 적 있나요?

1 Fill in the blanks with the correct words from the box. One word will not be used.

1 Many people around the world drink ___________ water.

2 Making bottles wastes a lot of water, energy, and _________.

3 Some experts say tap water is ___________.

2 After reading the article, circle T(true) or F(false).

1 Bottled water never has microplastics.　　　　T　F

2 Many people use these bottles one time and then throw them away.　　T　F

3 Complete the main idea sentence with words from the box.

Using ____________ water and tumblers instead of bottled water helps protect our ___________ and the Earth.

※ reusable 재사용할 수 있는   landfill (쓰레기) 매립지

1 drink / many people around the world / bottled water

____

전 세계에서 많은 사람들이 생수(플라스틱 병에 든 물)를 마셔요.

2 wastes / oil, water, and energy / a lot of / but / making bottles

____

하지만 병들을 만드는 것은 많은 기름, 물, 그리고 에너지를 낭비합니다.

3 safe / the water inside the bottles / even worse, / may not be

____

더 나쁜 것은, 병들 안에 있는 물이 안전하지 않을 수도 있어요.

4 93% of bottled water / microplastics / has / a study found that

In 2021,
____

2021년에, 한 연구는 생수의 93%가 미세 플라스틱을 가지고 있다는 것을 발견했어요.

5 a safer choice / is / some experts / tap water / say / because of this,

____

이것 때문에, 어떤 전문가들은 수돗물이 더 안전한 선택지라고 말합니다.

6 many people / these bottles once / use / and then throw them away

In addition,
____

게다가, 많은 사람들이 이 병들을 한 번 사용하고는 버려요.

7 a tumbler instead / using / can help reduce / so / waste

____

그래서 대신 텀블러를 사용하는 것이 쓰레기를 줄이는 데 도움이 됩니다.

8 help / our health / both / small changes like these / and the Earth

____

이런 작은 변화들이 우리의 건강과 지구 둘 다를 도와줘요.

← Step 2는 앞 쪽의 기사를 보고 답을 맞춰 보세요.

- plastics
- reduce
- resources
- actions
- environmental
- instead

Main Idea Bottled water causes ______________ problems and may be bad for people's health.

Details

1 Making bottles uses a lot of _________, such as oil and water.

2 Most bottled water has tiny _______, so tap water may be safer.

3 They also make a lot of waste, so using a tumbler can help ____________ waste.

Conclusion These ____________ can help the planet and our health.

※ resources 자원 action 행동, 실천 cause ~을 일으키다

STEP
04 토론하기 Choose and circle the correct answers.

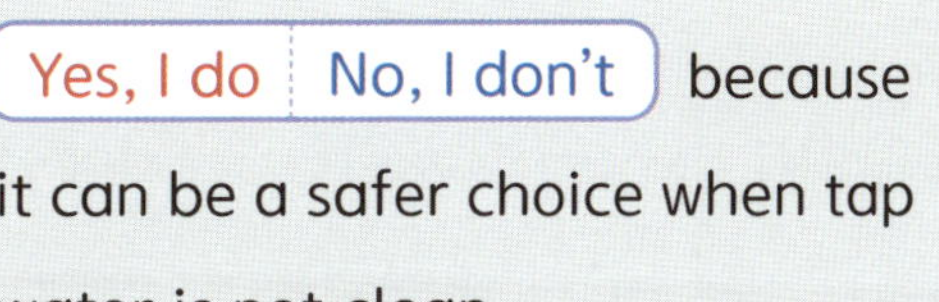

Should Kids Use AI for Homework?

Many students now use AI to get help with their homework. AI chatbots give answers very quickly. Some kids even ask AI to do all their homework. This can stop them from thinking on their own. Scientists say using AI too much hurts memory. One study found students using AI had 30% less brain activity while doing their homework. Therefore, it is best if students use AI only a little when needed. Using AI wisely is an important skill for students today.

Word Bank

AI(artificial intelligence) 인공지능

chatbot 채팅 로봇

on one's own 혼자서, 스스로

memory 기억력

brain 뇌

activity 활동

therefore 그러므로

유럽연합(EU) 일부 나라에서는 학교에서의 AI 사용 규칙을 정하기 시작했어요. 어떤 곳은 시험에서 AI 사용을 금지하고, 어떤 곳은 수업 도구로 활용하고 있어요. 나라별로 다른 방식을 비교하며 더 나은 방향을 찾으려는 시도도 있어요. 친구들은 우리나라 학교에서는 AI 사용과 관련하여 어떤 규칙이 필요하다고 생각하나요?

STEP 01 확인하기 Read and answer.

1 Fill in the blanks with the correct words from the box. One word will not be used.

quickly	own	homework	help

1. Many students ask AI for __________ with their homework.
2. Some kids make AI do all their ____________.
3. This can keep them from thinking on their __________.

2 After reading the article, circle T(true) or F(false).

1. AI chatbots give answers very quickly. T F
2. Getting help from AI with homework is never good. T F

3 Complete the main idea sentence with words from the box.

AI	machines	answers	skills

Students need to develop _________ to use _________ wisely when doing their homework.

※ skill 기술, 능력

1 now use / to get help / AI / with their homework / many students

____

많은 학생들이 요즘 숙제를 하는 데 도움을 받기 위해 AI를 사용해요.

2 give / AI chatbots / very quickly / answers

____

AI 챗봇들은 아주 빠르게 답을 줘요.

3 all their homework / even ask AI / some kids / to do

____

어떤 아이들은 심지어 AI에게 그들의 모든 숙제를 하도록 요청해요.

4 from thinking / can stop them / on their own / this

____

이것은 그들이 자기 자신의 힘으로 생각하는 것을 막을 수 있어요.

5 using AI / scientists say / too much / memory / hurts

____

과학자들은 AI를 너무 많이 사용하는 것이 기억력을 해친다고 말합니다.

6 had / while doing their homework / 30% less / students using AI / brain activity

One study found

한 연구는 AI를 사용하는 학생들이 숙제를 하는 동안 뇌 활동이 30% 더 적었다고 발견했어요.

7 it is best / therefore, / if students / when needed / use AI only a little

____

그러므로, 학생들이 필요할 때만 AI를 조금 사용하는 것이 가장 좋습니다.

8 is / for students today / an important skill / AI wisely / using

____

AI를 현명하게 사용하는 것은 오늘날 학생들에게 중요한 기술이에요.

← Step 2는 앞 쪽의 기사를 보고 답을 맞춰 보세요.

- students
- small
- activity
- avoid
- weaker
- wisely

Main Idea Students should use AI just a _____________ amount when they need help.

Details

1. AI is used by many ___________ for homework.
2. Some kids ___________ doing any homework themselves.
3. But too much use of AI can make their memories become ___________.

Conclusion For students today, it is important to learn how to use AI _______.

※ avoid 피하다 amount 양

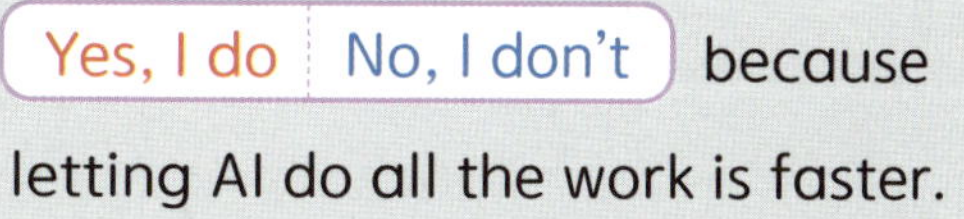

Word Bank

delivery 배달

create 만들어내다

package 택배 상자

layer 겹, 층

wrapping 포장재

pollution 오염

generate 발생시키다, 만들어내다

billion 10억

greenhouse gas 온실 가스

Fast Delivery, Big Problem

Online shopping is easy and fast. But it creates lots of waste from boxes and plastic. One package can use three layers of wrapping. More delivery trucks also cause more air pollution. In 2022, online shopping generated over 3 billion packages in Korea. This adds to greenhouse gas problems. Buying fewer things helps the Earth. Smart shopping makes a big difference for the environment.

⭐ 한국에서는 하루에 약 7천만 개의 택배 상자가 사용된다고 해요. 상자와 함께 비닐, 테이프, 완충재가 쓰이는데, 이런 재료들은 재활용이 쉽지 않아요. 쓰레기가 쌓이면서 분리수거 시설과 수거 인력에도 점점 더 큰 부담이 되고 있어요. 친구들은 택배 쓰레기를 줄이기 위해 어떤 노력을 시작하면 좋을거라고 생각하나요?

1 Fill in the blanks with the correct words from the box. One word will not be used.

> ○ waste   ○ Earth   ○ gas   ○ packages

1 Online shopping makes a lot of ___________ from boxes and wrapping.

2 In 2022, over 3 billion ___________ were generated in Korea.

3 Buying fewer things is good for the ___________.

2 After reading the article, circle T(true) or F(false).

1 Packages never have wrapping inside.   T   F

2 Delivery trucks add more pollution to the air.   T   F

3 Complete the main idea sentence with words from the box.

> ○ recycle   ○ shopping   ○ plastic   ○ pollution

Online ______________ creates a lot of waste and air ______________.

1 easy and fast / is / online shopping

____

온라인 쇼핑은 쉽고 빨라요.

2 creates / it / but / from boxes and plastic / lots of waste

____

하지만 그것은 상자들과 플라스틱으로부터 많은 쓰레기를 만들어내요.

3 can use / one package / of wrapping / three layers

____

하나의 택배 상자는 세 겹의 포장재를 사용할 수 있어요.

4 delivery trucks / more / also cause / air pollution / more

____

더 많은 배달 트럭들은 또한 더 많은 대기 오염을 일으켜요.

5 generated / online shopping / in Korea / over 3 billion packages

In 2022, ______________________________________

2022년에, 온라인 쇼핑은 한국에서 30억 개가 넘는 택배 상자들을 만들어냈습니다.

6 greenhouse gas problems / adds to / this

____

이것은 온실 가스 문제를 증가시켜요.

7 the Earth / fewer things / buying / helps

____

더 적은 물건들을 사는 것은 지구를 도와요.

8 makes / for the environment / a big difference / smart shopping

____

현명한 쇼핑은 환경에 큰 차이를 만듭니다.

← Step 2는 앞 쪽의 기사를 보고 답을 맞춰 보세요.

정리하기 Choose a word from the box and complete the organizer.

- harms
- layer
- delivery
- creates
- environment
- worse

Main Idea Online shopping ___________ the environment.

Details

1 Online shopping is easy and fast, but it ___________ lots of waste.

2 ___________ trucks can also pollute the air.

3 This makes greenhouse gas problems ___________.

Conclusion Making smart choices when shopping helps the ___________.

토론하기 Choose and circle the correct answers.

Do you agree with the **Main Idea** **?**

※ packaging 포장재

Smart Farms: The Future of Farming

Smart farms are growing in many parts of Korea. These farms use computers and sensors in greenhouses. The sensors check plant health every minute. The system controls light, air, and water by itself. It also controls harmful insects before they hurt the plants. Because of this, farmers use about 80% less pesticide. This helps them grow healthy plants all year with less pollution. Smart farms are changing the future of farming.

Word Bank

smart farm
스마트팜

sensor 센서, 감지 장치

greenhouse 온실

system 체계, 시스템

control
(벌레를) 막다, 조절하다

by itself 혼자서, 스스로

harmful 해로운

insect 곤충

pesticide 살충제, 농약

all year 일 년 내내

스마트팜은 기후 변화와 노동력 부족 문제를 해결하는 새로운 방법으로 주목받고 있어요. 한국에서는 스마트팜을 쓰는 농장에서 수확량이 일반 농장보다 30%나 더 늘었다고 해요. 또 물과 농약을 훨씬 적게 써서 지구를 지키는 데에도 도움이 된다고 해요. 친구들은 미래의 농장이 어떤 모습이면 좋을지 상상해 본 적 있나요?

1 Fill in the blanks with the correct words from the box. One word will not be used.

> ○ insects   ○ pesticide   ○ sensors   ○ itself

(1) Smart farms use computers and ___________.

(2) The system changes light, air, and water by ___________.

(3) It also controls harmful ___________ before the plants get hurt.

2 After reading the article, circle **T**(true) or **F**(false).

(1) Many areas in Korea now have more smart farms.   T   F

(2) Farmers use more pesticide on smart farms.   T   F

3 Complete the main idea sentence with words from the box.

> ○ farmers   ○ in summer   ○ cooks   ○ all year

Smart farms let _____________ grow healthy plants _____________ and make less pollution.

✻ cook 요리사

1 of Korea / are growing / smart farms / in many parts

____

스마트팜들은 한국의 많은 지역에서 늘어나고 있어요.

2 use / these farms / in greenhouses / computers and sensors

____

이 농장들은 온실 안에서 컴퓨터들과 센서들을 사용해요.

3 check / every minute / plant health / the sensors

____

그 센서들은 매 분마다 식물의 건강을 확인해요.

4 controls / the system / by itself / light, air, and water

____

그 시스템은 스스로 빛, 공기, 그리고 물을 조절합니다.

5 also controls / it / harmful insects / they hurt the plants / before

____

그것은 또한 해로운 벌레들이 식물들을 해치기 전에 막아요.

6 pesticide / use / farmers / about 80% less / because of this,

____

이것 때문에, 농부들은 약 80% 더 적은 농약을 사용합니다.

7 with less pollution / helps them grow / healthy plants all year / this

____

이것은 그들이 오염을 줄이면서 일 년 내내 건강한 식물들을 기르는 것을 도와줘요.

8 of farming / are changing / smart farms / the future

____

스마트팜들은 농사의 미래를 바꾸고 있어요.

← Step 2는 앞 쪽의 기사를 보고 답을 맞춰 보세요.

정리하기 Choose a word from the box and complete the organizer.

- pesticide
- automatically
- farming
- check
- technology
- year

Main Idea Smart farms can grow plants at any time of the ___________ with less pollution.

Details
1 Smart farms use ______________ to help plants grow.
2 The system ______________ controls light, air, and water.
3 It also controls harmful insects, so farmers use less ________.

Conclusion Smart farms are changing the future of ______________.

※ automatically 자동으로

토론하기 Choose and circle the correct answers.

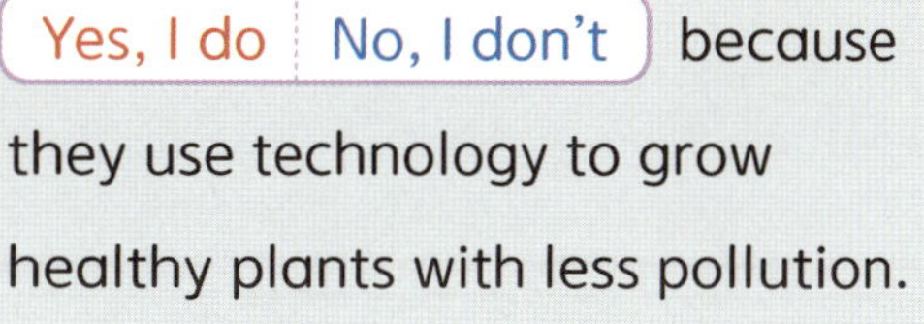

The Truth about Palm Oil

Palm oil is used in snacks, soap, and many other things. It is cheap and easy to make. But making palm oil destroys rainforests. Rainforests are homes for many animals. About 100,000 orangutans disappeared over the past 16 years. To help, we can choose items that don't use palm oil. Check ingredient labels carefully when you shop. Smart shopping helps protect the Earth and animals.

Word Bank

palm oil 팜유
(야자나무 열매에서
나오는 기름)

destroy 파괴하다

rainforest 열대 우림

orangutan 오랑우탄

disappear 사라지다

over ~ 동안, ~에 걸쳐

past 지난

ingredient
재료, 성분

label 라벨, 표지

유엔(UN)과 여러 나라들은 열대 우림을 보호하기 위해 '지속 가능한 팜유'라는 기준을 만들었어요. 이 기준을 지키는 농장은 나무를 무분별하게 베지 않고, 환경을 해치지 않도록 관리해요. 하지만 아직 참여하지 않는 농장도 많아서 산림 파괴는 계속되고 있어요. 친구들은 나라와 사람들이 힘을 모아 어떤 노력을 하면 좋겠다고 생각하나요?

1 Fill in the blanks with the correct words from the box. One word will not be used.

1 Snacks, soap, and many other things use ______________.

2 Making palm oil ______________ rainforests.

3 Check the ingredient ____________ of the items you buy.

2 After reading the article, circle T(true) or F(false).

1 Palm oil is expensive and difficult to make.   T F

2 Many animals, including orangutans, live in rainforests.   T F

3 Complete the main idea sentence with words from the box.

protect   without   with   destroy

We can choose products ______________ palm oil to help ______________ animals and the Earth.

✺ product 제품

1 is used / and many other things / in snacks, soap, / palm oil

____

팜유는 과자, 비누, 그리고 많은 다른 것들에 사용됩니다.

2 cheap / is / and easy to make / it

____

그것은 값이 싸고 만들기 쉬워요.

3 rainforests / making palm oil / but / destroys

____

하지만 팜유를 만드는 것은 열대 우림을 파괴해요.

4 are / for many animals / homes / rainforests

____

열대 우림은 많은 동물들의 집입니다.

5 disappeared / about 100,000 orangutans / the past 16 years / over

____

지난 16년 동안 약 100,000마리의 오랑우탄이 사라졌습니다.

6 palm oil / that don't use / we can choose / to help, / items

____

도움이 되기 위해, 우리는 팜유를 사용하지 않는 물건들을 선택할 수 있어요.

7 when you shop / ingredient labels carefully / check

____

당신이 쇼핑할 때, 성분 라벨들을 주의 깊게 확인하세요.

8 helps protect / and animals / the Earth / smart shopping

____

똑똑한 쇼핑은 지구와 동물들을 보호하는 것을 도와줘요.

← Step 2는 앞 쪽의 기사를 보고 답을 맞춰 보세요.

정리하기 Choose a word from the box and complete the organizer.

- rainforests
- hurts
- ingredient
- disappeared
- soap
- wildlife

 **Main Idea** Making palm oil ___________ nature and animals.

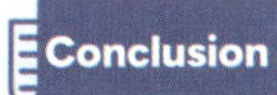 **Details**

1 It destroys ____________ where many animals live.

2 Many orangutans ____________ in the past 16 years.

3 To help, we can buy things that don't use palm oil as an ____________.

Conclusion Careful shopping choices can protect rainforests and ___________.

※ wildlife 야생 동물

토론하기 Choose and circle the correct answers.

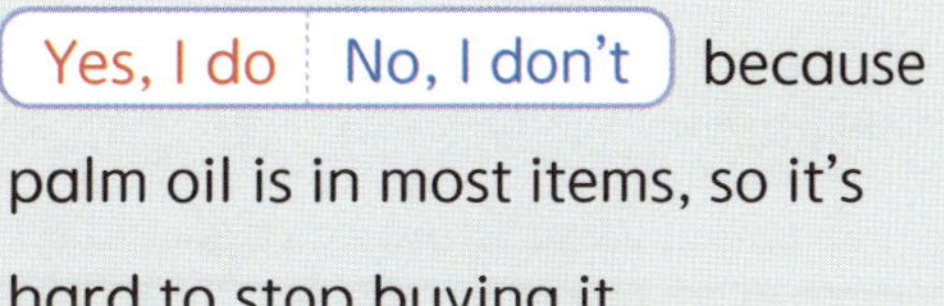

※ free ~이 없는

Word Bank

possibility 가능성

smart glasses
스마트 안경

than ever
(지금까지) 어느 때보다도

AR(augmented reality) 증강 현실

daily 일상적인

wearable device
웨어러블 디바이스
(몸에 착용할 수 있는
스마트 기기)

spread 퍼지다

New Glasses, New Possibilities

Smart glasses are back and better than ever. They now have cameras and small screens. These glasses use AR, or augmented reality. AR adds images to what you see in the real world. In 2024, Apple and Meta made new smart glasses for daily use. Experts say AR can help people learn and work in new ways. These wearable devices may spread to schools and hospitals soon. Smart glasses may soon be part of our daily lives.

★ 스마트 안경은 학교나 병원뿐 아니라 여러 분야에서 활용될 수 있다고 해요. 예를 들어 건축 현장에서는 3D 설계를 눈앞에서 확인하며 일할 수 있고, 여행 중에는 외국어 번역 자막을 바로 볼 수도 있어요. 이렇게 우리의 일상과 직업 세계에서 점점 더 큰 역할을 하게 될 스마트 안경, 친구들이라면 어떤 분야에서 가장 먼저 사용해 보고 싶나요?

1 Fill in the blanks with the correct words from the box. One word will not be used.

> • better   • AR   • work   • glasses

(1) Smart ___________ now have cameras and small screens.

(2) These glasses use ___________, or augmented reality.

(3) People can learn and ___________ in new ways with smart glasses.

2 After reading the article, circle **T**(true) or **F**(false).

(1) Smart glasses are back but worse than ever.   T F

(2) These glasses may be used in schools and hospitals.   T F

3 Complete the main idea sentence with words from the box.

> • less   • daily life   • more   • wearable devices

Soon, people might start using smart glasses ___________ often in ___________.

1 and better than ever / are back / smart glasses

스마트 안경은 돌아왔고, 이전 그 어느 때보다 더 좋아요.

2 and small screens / now have / they / cameras

그것들은 이제 카메라들과 작은 화면들을 가지고 있어요.

3 use AR, / these glasses / or augmented reality

이 안경들은 AR, 즉 증강 현실을 사용해요.

4 in the real world / adds images / AR / to what you see

AR은 당신이 실제 세계에서 보는 것에 이미지들을 더해요.

5 Apple and Meta / in 2024, / made / for daily use / new smart glasses

2024년에, 애플과 메타는 일상에서 사용하기 위한 새로운 스마트 안경을 만들었습니다.

6 can help people / AR / in new ways / learn and work / experts say

전문가들은 AR이 사람들이 새로운 방식들로 배우고 일하도록 도울 수 있다고 말합니다.

7 may spread / these wearable devices / soon / to schools and hospitals

이 웨어러블 디바이스들은 곧 학교들과 병원들로 퍼질지도 몰라요.

8 our daily lives / may soon be / smart glasses / part of

스마트 안경은 곧 우리의 일상생활의 일부가 될 수도 있어요.

← Step 2는 앞 쪽의 기사를 보고 답을 맞춰 보세요.

- daily
- everyday life
- change
- images
- spread
- wearable devices

 **Main Idea** Smart glasses may ___________ how people learn and work.

 **Details**

1 AR helps smart glasses add _________ to what people see in reality.

2 In 2024, Apple and Meta made smart glasses for people to use _________.

3 Schools and hospitals may soon start using ______________.

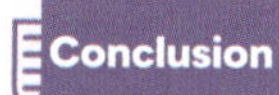 **Conclusion** Smart glasses could become something people use in __________ _________ soon.

※ daily 매일, 날마다   everyday life 일상생활   reality 현실

STEP **04** 토론하기 Choose and circle the correct answers.

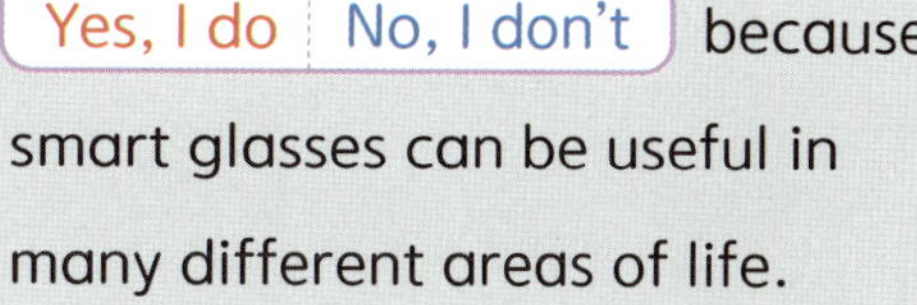

※ area 분야

Word Bank

in danger
위험에 처한

building 건물

smartphone
스마트폰

oil 석유

permission
허락, 허가

wisely 현명하게

Sand in Danger

Sand is not just for beaches and playgrounds. We need sand to make buildings, glass, and smartphones. Without sand, we cannot make many things we use every day. The world uses more sand than oil each year. Now, clean sand is harder to find in many places. Some people take sand from beaches without permission. This makes land smaller and hurts sea animals. We must save and use sand wisely to protect the Earth.

어떤 지역에서는 사람들이 허가 없이 해변이나 강에서 모래를 몰래 퍼 가기도 해요. 이렇게 되면 해안선이 줄어들고 땅이 약해져서 집이나 마을이 위험해질 수 있어요. 불법 채취는 자연뿐 아니라 그곳에 사는 사람들의 삶에 심각한 영향을 미친다고 해요. 친구들은 모래를 지키기 위해 어떤 규칙이나 제도가 필요하다고 생각하나요?

1 Fill in the blanks with the correct words from the box. One word will not be used.

> ○ without   ○ oil   ○ sand   ○ playgrounds

1 We use ___________ to make buildings, glass, and smartphones.

2 We can't make many things we use every day ___________ sand.

3 People around the world use more sand than ___________.

2 After reading the article, circle T(true) or F(false).

1 Clean sand is now easier to find in many places.   T   F

2 Some people take sand from beaches without asking.   T   F

3 Complete the main idea sentence with words from the box.

> ○ demand   ○ many   ○ enough   ○ permission

The _______________ for sand is high, but the world may not have ___________ sand.

✽ demand 수요(어떤 물건을 사거나 쓰고 싶어 하는 필요와 양)

1 beaches and playgrounds / is not just for / sand

모래는 해변들이나 놀이터들을 위한 것만은 아니에요.

2 need sand / we / buildings, glass, and smartphones / to make

우리는 건물들, 유리, 그리고 스마트폰들을 만들기 위해 모래가 필요해요.

3 cannot make / we use every day / many things / without sand, / we

모래가 없으면, 우리는 우리가 매일 사용하는 많은 물건들을 만들 수 없어요.

4 uses / the world / more sand / each year / than oil

세계는 매년 석유보다 더 많은 모래를 사용합니다.

5 in many places / clean sand / now, / is harder to find

지금은, 깨끗한 모래는 많은 장소들에서 찾기가 더 어려워요.

6 take sand / without permission / from beaches / some people

어떤 사람들은 허가 없이 해변에서 모래를 가져가요.

7 makes land / this / and hurts / smaller / sea animals

이것은 땅을 더 작게 만들고 바다 동물들을 해쳐요.

8 must save and use / we / to protect the Earth / sand wisely

우리는 지구를 보호하기 위해 모래를 아끼고 현명하게 사용해야 합니다.

← Step 2는 앞 쪽의 기사를 보고 답을 맞춰 보세요.

- more
- permission
- saving
- less
- daily life
- glass

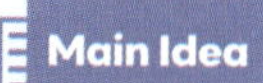 **Main Idea** We need sand for many things in _______________.

 **Details**

1 People use sand to make _______, smartphones, and buildings.

2 Every year, _________ sand is used than oil.

3 People sometimes take sand without ____________, and this harms sea animals.

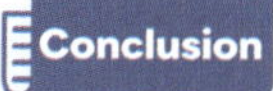 **Conclusion** _________ and using sand wisely can help protect the Earth.

✹ daily life 일상생활

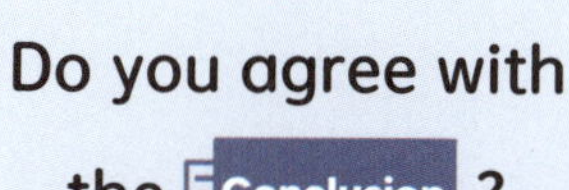

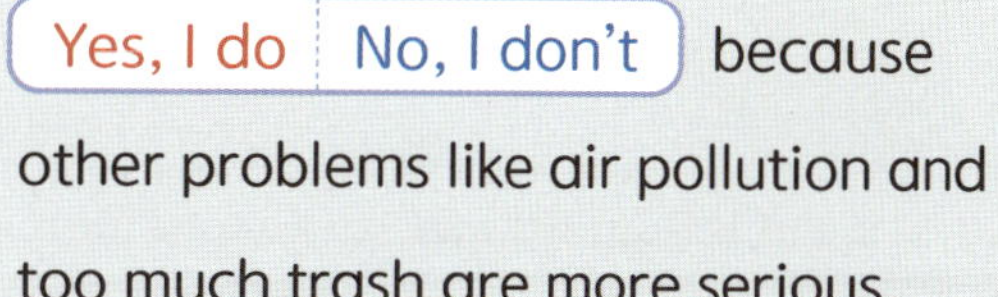

Holes under Our Feet

Sinkholes are becoming more common in many cities. For example, Seoul had over 90 sinkholes in one year. Because of this, scientists check the ground with radar for empty spaces. This radar sends signals back and shows weak areas. Satellites also help check if the land is moving. Another method is to make a small hole and to test the ground. With these tests, experts can fix weak ground early. Science is helping keep people safe from sinkholes.

Word Bank

sinkhole 싱크홀
(땅이 꺼져 생기는 큰 구멍)

common
흔한, 자주 있는

radar 레이더
(전파를 이용해 물체의 위치를 알아내는 장치)

empty 빈

space 공간

signal 신호

satellite 위성

method 방법

⭐ 싱크홀은 갑자기 땅이 꺼져서 큰 피해를 줄 수 있어요. 그래서 과학자들은 다양한 기술을 사용해 미리 위험을 찾는다고 해요. 예를 들어 지하를 스캔하는 레이더는 땅속 빈 공간을 보여주고, 위성은 땅이 조금씩 움직이는지도 관찰할 수 있어요. 또 작은 구멍을 뚫어 토양을 검사하는 방법도 쓰이고 있어요. 만약 친구들이 과학자라면 싱크홀을 방지하기 위해 어떤 새로운 기술을 만들어 보고 싶나요?

1 Fill in the blanks with the correct words from the box. One word will not be used.

> ○ moving   ○ space   ○ radar   ○ sinkholes

(1) Seoul had over 90 ______________ in one year.

(2) Scientists check the ground by using ____________ to find weak areas.

(3) Satellites also help see if the land is ____________.

2 After reading the article, circle T(true) or F(false).

(1) Sinkholes are becoming less common in many cities.   T F

(2) Experts use different tests to keep people safe from sinkholes.   T F

3 Complete the main idea sentence with words from the box.

> ○ happen   ○ signal   ○ underground   ○ find

Science helps experts __________ and fix weak ground before sinkholes __________.

※ underground 지하의

1 are becoming / in many cities / more common / sinkholes

____

싱크홀들은 많은 도시들에서 점점 더 흔해지고 있어요.

2 in one year / had / Seoul / over 90 sinkholes / for example,

____

예를 들어, 서울에서는 1년 동안 90개가 넘는 싱크홀이 생겼습니다.

3 check the ground / with radar / scientists / for empty spaces

Because of this, ____

이것 때문에, 과학자들은 빈 공간들을 (찾기) 위해 레이더로 땅을 확인해요.

4 sends / this radar / signals back / weak areas / and shows

____

이 레이더는 신호들을 다시 보내고 약한 지역들을 보여줘요.

5 is moving / also help check / satellites / if the land

____

위성들은 또한 땅이 움직이고 있는지를 확인하는 것을 도와줘요.

6 to make / is / another method / and to test the ground / a small hole

____

또 다른 방법은 작은 구멍을 만들고 땅을 테스트하는 거예요.

7 experts / weak ground / can fix / early / with these tests,

____

이런 테스트들로, 전문가들은 약한 땅을 일찍 고칠 수 있습니다.

8 is helping / science / from sinkholes / keep people safe

____

과학은 사람들이 싱크홀들로부터 안전하도록 돕고 있습니다.

← Step 2는 앞 쪽의 기사를 보고 답을 맞춰 보세요.

정리하기 Choose a word from the box and complete the organizer.

- empty
- danger
- methods
- hole
- protect
- satellites

Main Idea Different scientific _______________ are used to find sinkholes.

Details
1. Radar helps experts find __________ spaces below the ground.
2. Scientists use _______________ to see if the land is moving.
3. Another way is to make a small __________ and to check the ground.

Conclusion Science helps __________ people from sinkholes.

※ danger 위험 scientific 과학적인

토론하기 Choose and circle the correct answers.

Do you agree with the **Conclusion**?

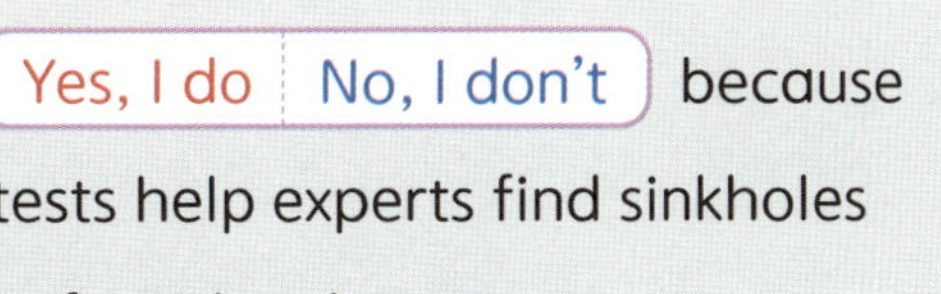

Word Bank

recycle 재활용하다

recycling bin 재활용 통

waste 폐기물, 쓰레기

mixed 섞인

as a result 그 결과로

label 라벨, 표시

responsible 책임 있는

Clean and Check before Recycling

Many people think all trash in recycling bins gets recycled. But some waste can't be recycled because it is mixed. For example, some cups have both plastic and paper. Some items are too dirty to recycle. As a result, most of it gets burned instead. A 2022 study says only 9% of plastic is recycled. We must check labels and clean items before recycling. Better recycling starts with responsible habits at home.

⭐ 한국은 재활용률이 높다고 알려져 있지만, 실제로는 플라스틱의 절반 이상이 재활용되지 않는다고 해요. 특히 음식물이 묻은 용기는 대부분 태워지거나 땅에 묻히게 돼요. 그래서 깨끗하게 분리수거하는 습관이 아주 중요해요. 친구들은 우리가 어떻게 하면 재활용되는 양을 더 늘릴 수 있다고 생각하나요?

1 Fill in the blanks with the correct words from the box. One word will not be used.

> ○ dirty   ○ recycled   ○ plastic   ○ check

(1) Some waste cannot be _______________ since it is mixed.

(2) Items that are too ___________ cannot be recycled.

(3) A study in 2022 said just 9% of ___________ was recycled.

2 After reading the article, circle T(true) or F(false).

(1) All the waste in recycling bins is recycled.　　　T　F

(2) Some cups cannot be recycled because they have both plastic and paper.　　　T　F

3 Complete the main idea sentence with words from the box.

> ○ reuse   ○ responsible   ○ careless   ○ recycling

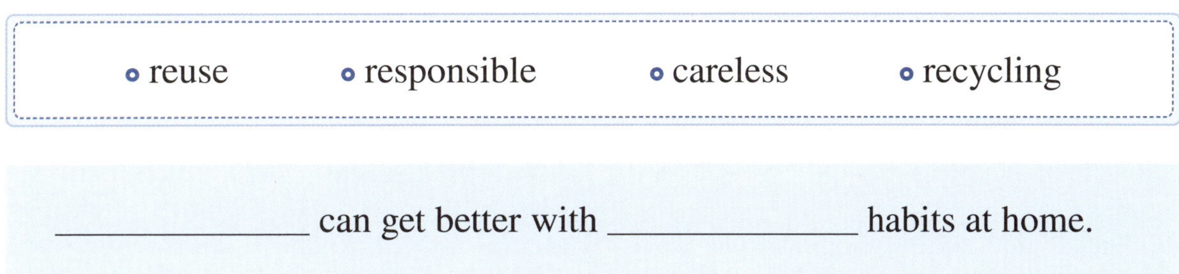

_______________ can get better with _______________ habits at home.

※ reuse 재사용하다   careless 부주의한

1 think / many people / gets recycled / in recycling bins / all trash

많은 사람들은 재활용 통 안에 있는 모든 쓰레기가 재활용된다고 생각해요.

2 can't be recycled / mixed / some waste / but / because it is

하지만 어떤 쓰레기는 섞여 있기 때문에 재활용될 수 없어요.

3 both plastic and paper / some cups / for example, / have

예를 들어, 어떤 컵들은 플라스틱과 종이를 둘 다 가지고 있어요.

4 are / to recycle / too dirty / some items

어떤 물건들은 재활용하기에 너무 더러워요.

5 most of it / as a result, / instead / gets burned

그 결과로, 그것(쓰레기)의 대부분은 대신 태워집니다.

6 is recycled / says / only 9% of plastic / a 2022 study

2022년의 한 연구는 플라스틱의 오직 9%만 재활용된다고 말합니다.

7 must check labels / we / before recycling / and clean items

우리는 재활용하기 전에 라벨들을 확인하고 물건들을 깨끗이 해야 해요.

8 at home / starts / better recycling / with responsible habits

더 나은 재활용은 집에서의 책임 있는 습관들로 시작됩니다.

← Step 2는 앞 쪽의 기사를 보고 답을 맞춰 보세요.

03 정리하기 **Choose a word from the box and complete the organizer.**

> - materials
> - check
> - recycled
> - burn
> - home
> - clean

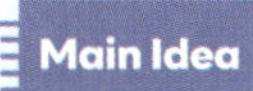 **Main Idea** Not all trash in recycling bins gets ______________.

 **Details**

1 Some waste ____________ are mixed and cannot be recycled.

2 Some items are not ____________ enough to be recycled.

3 We should __________ labels and wash them before recycling.

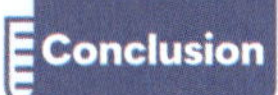 **Conclusion** Better recycling begins with what we do at ____________.

❊ material 재질, 재료

STEP

04 토론하기 **Choose and circle the correct answers.**

Do you agree with the **Conclusion**?

Word Bank

diet 다이어트

shot 주사

obesity 비만

lose weight
체중을 줄이다, 살을 빼다

hormone 호르몬

fatty 기름진

throw up 토하다

work best
가장 좋은 효과를 내다

daily 일상적인

medicine 약

Diet Shots vs. Healthy Habits

Obesity is a growing problem in many parts of the world. To fight obesity, doctors now give diet shots to help people lose weight. In 2023, about 5 million people around the world used them. They work by making the brain send out a hormone. It makes people less hungry and want less fatty food. But many people who use them can feel sick or throw up. Doctors say healthy food, exercise, and sleep work best. Healthy daily habits are still the best medicine.

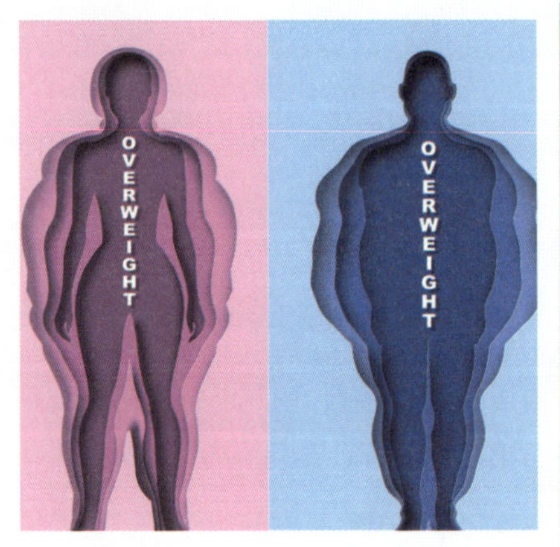

⭐ 세계보건기구(WHO)에 따르면, 전 세계 비만율은 수십 년 동안 두 배 이상 늘어났고 한국에서도 비만율이 계속 올라가고 있다고 해요. 요즘은 다이어트 주사가 많이 쓰이고 있지만, 의사들은 주사보다 건강한 식습관, 꾸준한 운동, 그리고 충분한 수면이 가장 좋은 해결책이라고 해요. 친구들은 건강을 위해 어떤 생활 습관을 꼭 지키고 싶나요?

1 Fill in the blanks with the correct words from the box. One word will not be used.

> ○ hormone   ○ weight   ○ food   ○ exercise

① These days, doctors use diet shots to help people lose ___________.

② The shots make the brain send out a ___________.

③ The hormone makes people want less fatty ___________.

2 After reading the article, circle T(true) or F(false).

① Obesity is becoming a big problem worldwide.   T F

② Diet shots are the best medicine because they are always safe.   T F

3 Complete the main idea sentence with words from the box.

> ○ obesity   ○ hungry   ○ side effects   ○ habits

Diet shots have ________________, so healthy ___________ are still the best choice.

❋ side effect 부작용

기사 쓰기 Unscramble the sentences below.

1 a growing problem / is / of the world / in many parts / obesity

비만은 세계 많은 지역들에서 점점 커지는 문제예요.

2 diet shots / now give / doctors / lose weight / to help people

To fight obesity,

비만을 줄이기 위해, 의사들은 요즘 사람들에게 살을 빼도록 돕는 다이어트 주사를 줘요.

3 used them / about 5 million people / in 2023, / around the world

2023년에, 전 세계에서 약 500만 명의 사람들이 그것들(다이어트 주사)을 사용했습니다.

4 work / they / a hormone / send out / by making the brain

그것들은 뇌가 호르몬을 내보내도록 만듦으로써 효과를 내요.

5 and want / makes people / less hungry / it / less fatty food

그것(호르몬)은 사람들이 덜 배고프고 기름진 음식을 덜 원하게 만들어요.

6 who use them / but / or throw up / can feel sick / many people

하지만 그것들을 사용하는 많은 사람들이 아프거나 토할 수도 있어요.

7 and sleep / doctors say / healthy food, exercise, / work best

의사들은 건강한 음식, 운동, 그리고 수면이 가장 좋은 효과를 낸다고 말합니다.

8 are still / healthy daily habits / medicine / the best

건강한 일상 습관들이 여전히 최고의 약입니다.

← Step 2는 앞 쪽의 기사를 보고 답을 맞춰 보세요.

- sick
- obesity
- fast food
- exercising
- less
- lose

Main Idea Healthy habits are still better for treating __________ than diet shots.

Details

1 Doctors sometimes give people diet shots to help them __________ weight.

2 These shots help the brain send out a hormone that makes people want __________ food.

3 But many people who get them may feel __________.

Conclusion Eating healthy food, __________, and getting enough sleep work best.

※ fast food 패스트푸드   treat 치료하다

STEP
04 토론하기 Choose and circle the correct answers.

Do you agree with the **Main Idea**?

MEMO

바빠 영어신문

NEWS TIMES
뉴스 타임스

Dictation

① QR코드로 받아쓰기 음원을 듣고 빈칸에 단어를 채워 보세요.
② 정답을 확인한 후, 틀린 부분만 집중해서 다시 들어 보면 최고!

내가 틀린 문제를 스스로 정리하는 습관을 들이면, 시간이 오래 흘러도 계속 기억할 수 있어요!

Haeundae Beach Is Shrinking!

정답: 10쪽

Every summer, many people ______ Haeundae Beach.

However, the beach is slowly ______ ______.

Scientists say global warming ___ ______ sea levels.

Higher waves pull more sand into the ocean.

______ storms also cause heavy beach erosion.

Each year, Haeundae ______ around 2 meters of sand.

The city of Busan ______ ___ ______ more sand soon.

They hope this will ______ ______ the beach.

정답: 14쪽

Sleep Better with Less Screen Time

These days, kids often _______ _______ or _______ _______ before bed.

_______ _______ from screens _______ the brain think it is daytime.

This happens _______ it lowers a sleep hormone _______ melatonin.

In fact, blue light before bedtime _______ _______ melatonin by 55%.

Less melatonin makes it harder to _______ _______ at night.

Poor sleep can cause _______ _______ _______ _______.

Experts say to _______ _______ _______ screens one hour before bed.

This simple habit can _______ _______ better sleep.

When Cows Burp, the Earth Gets Hot

정답: 18쪽

__________ is a popular choice _____ _______ around the world.

But __________ _______ hurts the Earth when they _______.

The gas from these burps ___ ________ methane, and it ________ the Earth.

Research shows cows ___________ about 100 kilograms of methane _______ _____.

One way ____ ________ _____ __________ is ____ _________ the cows' food.

Adding _________ _______ like seaweed helps _______ ________ _____.

__________ _______ is to eat less beef and meat.

________ _____ __________ can help protect _____ _______.

Can We Find Life Beyond Earth?

정답: 22쪽

Many people __________ if life exists __________

__________ .

NASA sends robots to __________ __________ and to

__________ __________ __________ of life.

Right now, NASA ___ __________ Mars the most.

In 2021, NASA __________ ___ __________ called Perseverance

___ __________ .

After studying ________ , NASA wants to __________

__________ __________ .

One place that NASA __________ __________ ___ is

Europa, a moon of Jupiter.

Scientists believe ________ under Europa's ice may

__________ ___ .

__________ ___ would be a very __________

moment for __________ .

Plant-Based Meat: Good or Bad?

정답: 26쪽

More people _________ food that ___ _________ for our planet.

_________ _________ many people now choose _________ _________ _________.

This kind of meat is made _________ _________, _________ _________.

It uses _____ water and makes _____ pollution _________ animal meat.

For example, it uses 90% _____ _________ than making _____ _________.

But some people _________ that it is not good for _____ _________.

It can have _____ _________ salt or _____ _________ chemicals.

Even so, the _________ for plant-based meat ___ _________.

Can a Machine Catch a Lie?

정답: 30쪽

Lie detectors _____ __________ more common these days.

They _______ ___ body changes ________ questions.

When people lie or feel nervous, their hearts _______ _______.

They may also _________ faster and _______ ___ _______.

Police sometimes use ____ __________ when asking __________.

Some people worry that they _____ ____ _________ ______.

One study found that lie detectors ____ _______ about 30% of the time.

The machines ____ _______ but still need _________ ____.

음원 듣기

정답: 34쪽

A Fish That Eats Plastic!

A study says there are __________ __________ microplastics in the __________.

Although plastic pollution ___ __________ __________, there's good news.

Now, ___ __________ __________ can __________ them and __________ them ___.

It swims __________ ___ __________ __________ and eats plastic.

This robot can __________ 500 kilograms of waste.

It is __________ __________ __________ but very __________.

Scientists are testing it ___ __________, __________, __________.

Many people __________ __________ about this new technology.

Do Plants Talk?

In 2023, ____________ found that ________ make sounds.

These clicking ________ happen when plants are ______ or _________.

People _________ ______ the sounds _________ a special machine.

The stressed plants ________ over 40 times ___ _____ _____.

On the other hand, healthy plants made _____ ___ ____ _________.

Scientists _______ the sounds ______ other plants.

Other plants ______ the sounds and _______ changes ___ _______ _____.

Plant sounds could ______ ___ smarter farming ___ _____ _________.

Animals Need Quiet Homes, Too

정답: 42쪽

Today, _________ _________ live near people.

However, ______ ______ from cars and machines can _______ ______.

Some animals _______ their homes because of ______.

In the ocean, _____ ______ makes _________________ hard ____ _________.

One study says dolphins _________ _______________ well in loud places.

______ _________ make animals _______ or _________.

Some animals ______ _________ their babies.

It is time to ______ _______ how our noise _________ animals.

10 Can Humans Make Diamonds?

Now, _______ can make ____________ in just a few days.

This is _____ _______ because it _______ millions of years ____ _______ them in nature.

This makes ____________ diamonds ___ ____ _________.

That's _______ they are also ________ for many industries.

For example, they _______ ____ _______ in things like __________ __________ and ________ _______.

Because of this, many companies _____ ___________ lab diamonds today.

In 2023, _______ of lab diamonds _______ by 20%.

Lab diamonds _____ ___________ the future of science.

Food Waste Isn't Just about Food

정답: 50쪽

___ _________ ____ ________ says about 30% of food is wasted _________.

However, ___________ ______ is not just about food ______.

Food takes ______, ______, ____ ________ to grow.

We lose all of that _______ ______ ___ ________.

________ _____ the only problem.

Wasting food also ______ harmful gases ___ _____ ____.

This happens because _______ use _________, and _________ ______ burns _____.

That's why __________ ____ ______ is important for the ____________.

Fake Germs, Real Protection

________ COVID-19, more people ______ ___ ______ how vaccines work.

Our bodies have ____ ________ ______ that fights germs.

Vaccines help this system ______ ___ ______ ______.

They use ______ ___ _____ ______ to do this.

This helps the body learn ________ ________ ____.

After that, the immune system _________ the germs.

As a result, the body ______ them ______ _____ ______ next time.

That's why ________ _______ is a smart way to ________ your body.

응원 듣기

정답: 58쪽

Save Water, Save the World!

Water ___ _____________ _________ to find in many places.

This ___ _____________ because of _________ _________ and _________.

A global study _______ that 1 in 3 people _______ _______ _______ water.

This problem affects _______ _____ _____ _______ countries.

That's why everyone _________ _____.

At home, we can _______ ____ the water while _________ ____ _______.

Using a bowl ____ ______ fruits and vegetables helps, ____.

Small actions like these _____ ______ a lot of water.

14 Can Robots Feel Emotions?

Today, robots can show ___________ like humans.

They ________, talk ________, and even __________ ____ people's faces.

Many people _____ ___________ because these actions look real.

In 2023, ___ ________ _______ that 65% of people think robots ____________ feelings.

But robots ____ ____ _____ _____ emotions like humans.

They only _______ feelings by using data that they ________.

Their responses _____ ________ ____ _______, not real emotions.

Still, this helps them _______ ________ with people.

정답: 66쪽

Too Many Clothes, Too Much Waste

Fast fashion is __ __________ _________ around the world.

It means people buy ______ ___ ________ ________.

They wear these clothes ______ ___ _____ _______.

After that, they ________ the clothes away.

Each year, over 92 million tons of clothes _____ _________.

This ________ more pollution and _______ the planet.

To help, we can _______ clothes longer or _____ eco-friendly clothes.

______ _____ ________ and _____ clothes can help the planet.

16 No Driver, No Problem?

음원 듣기
정답: 70쪽

People around the world _______ _________ about

___________________ _______.

Self-driving cars can move __________ _________.

They use ___________, _________, ________ to drive.

In 2024, _______ ____ _______ tested this new technology.

The goal is to ______ people _______ more ________ in the future.

But _______ _________ worry about accidents and system errors.

_________ _________ what the cars will do in difficult situations.

We need ______ ______ and ______ ________ for the future.

The Earth Is Warming Too Fast

정답: 74쪽

____________ ____________ is warming ____________ ____________ ____________.

Global temperatures ____ ____ ____ 0.2°C every 10 years.

____________ ____________ seems small, but it is ____________ for life.

____________, ____________, ____________ may get worse.

Some plants and animals may ____________ forever.

Scientists also ____________ that if the Earth gets 1.5°C ____________, things will get ____________ ____________.

This means ____________ ____________ ____________ ____________ climate problems.

We need to help ____________ our planet before it's ____________ ____________.

18 Smarter Arms and Legs

정답: 78쪽

Bionic ____________ ______ ______ are getting __________.

They are machine parts that act like real arms and legs.

For example, some bionic arms can ______ __________ from the ________.

They let people ________ their arms just by __________.

Bionic legs are also __________ ________.

They have smart sensors to help __________ people ______ __________.

A study says they can ______ ________ the chances of falling by ________ ______.

These new changes ______ __________ hope to many people.

Fun Festivals, Big Trash

정답: 82쪽

Festivals bring __________, _______, ______ ______.

But they also create ___ ____ ____ _________.

________ _________ in Seoul _________ 50 tons of trash in 2022.

That's ___ ________ ___ 40 cars!

Because of this, _______________ events are getting _______ ___________.

For example, these events _____ _______ plastic items.

Some events ask _________ to bring their own cups.

It's a _______ but __________ step to help the _____________.

20 Is Nuclear Power Worth the Risk?

Many people want ________ ________ to save the Earth.

________ ________ makes a lot of energy ________ creating carbon gas.

One ________ ________ can give power to about 1 million homes.

But ________ like the one at Fukushima ________ people.

Nuclear waste also ________ ________ for thousands of years.

________ think it is not ________ the risk.

Others say ________ ________ it for clean energy.

________ ________ continues as we ________ climate change.

The Truth about Bottled Water

음원 듣기
정답: 90쪽

Many people around the world drink __________ __________.

But making bottles wastes a ____ ____ ____, ________, ______ ________.

Even worse, the water inside the bottles ______ ______ ____ ______.

In 2021, ___ ________ ________ that 93% of bottled water has ____________.

Because of this, some experts say ______ ________ is a safer ________.

In addition, many people use ______ ________ once and then ________ ______ ______.

So ________ ___ ________ instead can help ________ waste.

__________ __________ like these help both ______ and ____ ______.

Should Kids Use AI for Homework?

정답: 94쪽

Many students now _____ ___ to get help _____ their

______________.

AI chatbots ______ _________ very quickly.

Some kids even ask AI to ____ ____ ______

____________.

This _____ _____ them from thinking ____ ______

______.

Scientists say using AI too much hurts memory.

One study ________ students ______ ___ had 30%

less ______ _________ while doing their homework.

Therefore, __ __ ______ if students ____ ___ only a

little ______ _________.

Using AI ________ is an ____________ _____ for

_________ today.

Fast Delivery, Big Problem

______________ ____________ is easy and fast.

But it __________ lots of waste from ________ ______ ________.

One package can use _______ ________ of wrapping.

More delivery trucks also cause ________ _____ ___________.

In 2022, online shopping generated _______ ___ ________ ____________ in Korea.

This adds to _____________ _____ problems.

_________ _______ ________ helps the Earth.

_________ ___________ makes ___ ______ _____________ for the environment.

Smart Farms: The Future of Farming

정답: 102쪽

___________ ___________ are growing in many parts of ___________.

These farms use ___________ ___________ ___________ in greenhouses.

The sensors check ___________ health ___________ ___________.

The system controls ___________, ___________, ___________ ___________ by itself.

It also controls ___________ ___________ before they ___________ the plants.

Because of this, ___________ use ___________ ___________ ___________ pesticide.

This helps them grow ___________ ___________ all year with ___________ ___________.

Smart farms ___________ ___________ ___________ the future of farming.

The Truth about Palm Oil

음원 듣기
정답: 106쪽

________ ____ is used in snacks, soap, and many other things.

It is ________ _____ _____ to make.

But making palm oil _______ rainforests.

__________ are ______ for many animals.

About 100,000 orangutans __________ over the past ______.

To help, we can _______ _____ that don't use palm oil.

Check ________ _____ carefully when you _____.

Smart shopping _____ ______ the Earth and animals.

New Glasses, New Possibilities

Smart glasses _____ _____ ____ ______ than ever.

They now have ___________ ____ ______ ______ .

________ ________ use ____ , or augmented reality.

AR ______ _______ to what you see ___ ____ _____ ______ .

In 2024, Apple and Meta made _____ _______ _______ for daily use.

________ say AR can _____ ________ ______ and _____ in new ways.

These wearable devices _____ _______ to ________ ____ ________ soon.

Smart glasses may soon ___ ____ ___ _____ _____ ____ .

Sand in Danger

정답: 114쪽

Sand is not just for __________ and ________________.

We ______ ______ to make buildings, glass, and smartphones.

Without sand, we ________ ______ many things we use every day.

The world uses ______ ______ ______ ____ each year.

Now, clean sand __ ________ to find in many places.

Some people take ______ ______ ________ without ________.

This makes ______ ________ and hurts ____ ________.

We ________ ______ ____ sand wisely to ________ the Earth.

Holes under Our Feet

음원 듣기

정답: 118쪽

______________ are becoming ______ __________ in many cities.

______ __________ , Seoul had ______ ____ sinkholes in one year.

Because of this, ___________ check the ground with radar for ________ _________ .

This radar ________ signals back and shows ________ ________ .

Satellites also ______ _______ if the land ___ _________ .

_________ method is to make ___ ________ ______ and to ______ the ground.

______ these tests, _________ can fix weak ground ______ .

Science ___ _________ keep people ______ from sinkholes.

Clean and Check before Recycling

정답: 122쪽

Many people think _____ _______ in recycling bins _______ __________.

But some waste _______ ___ _________ because it ___ _______.

For example, some cups have both ________ and ________.

Some items are _____ ______ ___ ________.

As a result, most of it _____ ________ instead.

A 2022 study says _______ ____ ___ ________ is recycled.

We must _______ labels and _______ items before recycling.

________ __________ starts with ___________ ________ at home.

Diet Shots vs. Healthy Habits

____________ is a growing problem in ________ ________ of the world.

To fight obesity, _________ now give _____ _______ to help people _____ _______ .

In 2023, ________ ___ _______ ________ around the world used them.

They work by making _____ _______ send out ___ ___________ .

It makes people _____ _______ and want _____ ______ _____ .

But _______ ________ who use them can _____ _____ or ________ ____ .

Doctors say _________ _____, _________, _____ ______ work best.

________ daily habits are still _____ ______ ___________ .

MEMO

바빠 영어 신문

NEWS TIMES
뉴스 타임스

Answer

Haeundae Beach Is Shrinking!

S T E P 01

1 ① visit ② rise ③ sand

2 ① F ② T

3 smaller, fix

S T E P 03

Main Idea shrinking

Details ① summer ② sea levels ③ erosion

Conclusion protect

S T E P 04

1 Yes, I do   **2** No, I don't

02 **Science** 14쪽

Sleep Better with Less Screen Time

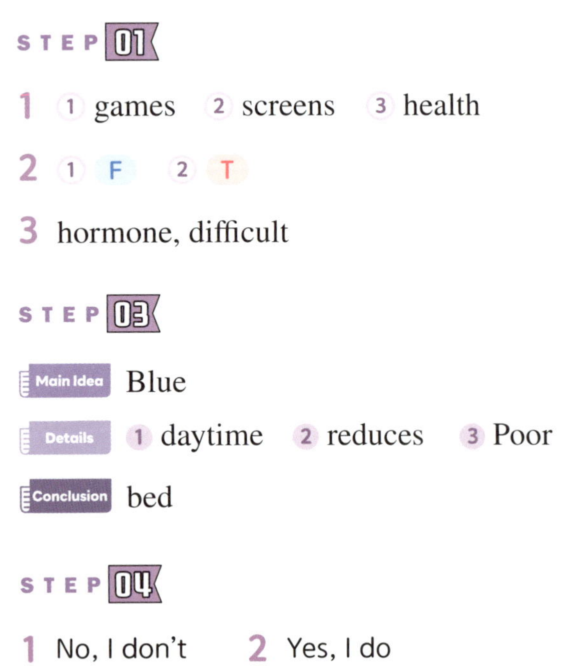

S T E P 01

1 ① games ② screens ③ health

2 ① F ② T

3 hormone, difficult

S T E P 03

Main Idea Blue

Details ① daytime ② reduces ③ Poor

Conclusion bed

S T E P 04

1 No, I don't   **2** Yes, I do

When Cows Burp, the Earth Gets Hot

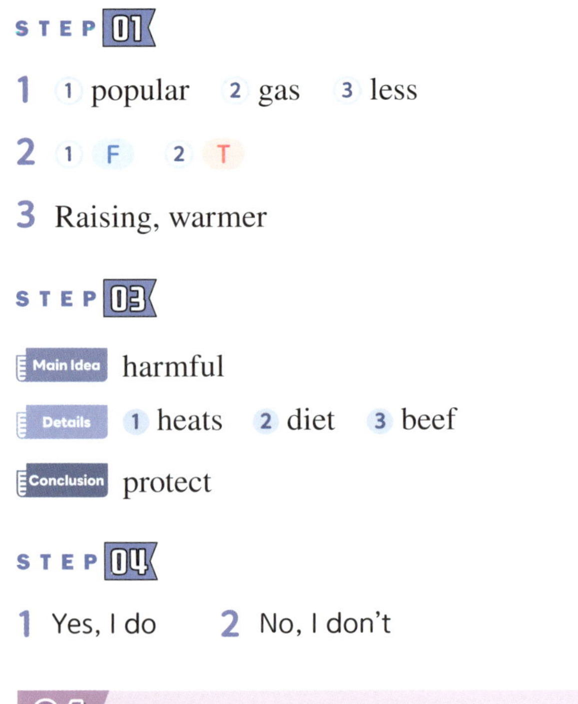

S T E P 01

1 ① popular ② gas ③ less

2 ① F ② T

3 Raising, warmer

S T E P 03

Main Idea harmful

Details ① heats ② diet ③ beef

Conclusion protect

S T E P 04

1 Yes, I do   **2** No, I don't

04 **Science** 22쪽

Can We Find Life Beyond Earth?

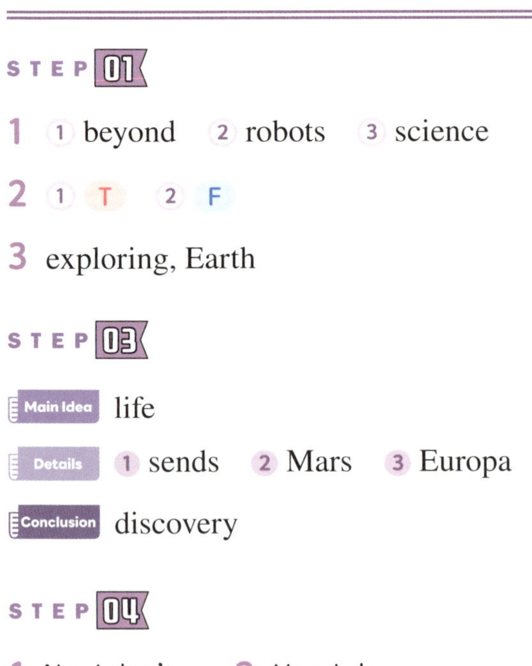

S T E P 01

1 ① beyond ② robots ③ science

2 ① T ② F

3 exploring, Earth

S T E P 03

Main Idea life

Details ① sends ② Mars ③ Europa

Conclusion discovery

S T E P 04

1 No, I don't   **2** Yes, I do

05   Environment   26쪽

Plant-Based Meat: Good or Bad?

STEP 01

1 ① Plant-based ② animals ③ chemicals

2 ① T ② F

3 plants, environment

STEP 03

Main Idea Earth

Details ① less ② unhealthy ③ salt

Conclusion market

STEP 04

1 Yes, I do 　2 No, I don't

---

06   Science   30쪽

Can a Machine Catch a Lie?

STEP 01

1 ① common ② sweat ③ Police

2 ① T ② F

3 catch, changes

STEP 03

Main Idea detect

Details ① questions ② breathe ③ mistakes

Conclusion carefully

STEP 04

1 No, I don't 　2 Yes, I do

---

07   Environment   34쪽

A Fish That Eats Plastic!

STEP 01

1 ① microplastics ② robot ③ light

2 ① T ② F

3 remove, environment

STEP 03

Main Idea fish-shaped

Details ① worse ② collects ③ lakes

Conclusion technology

STEP 04

1 Yes, I do 　2 No, I don't

---

08   Science   38쪽

Do Plants Talk?

STEP 01

1 ① machine ② healthy ③ safe

2 ① T ② F

3 pain, stress

STEP 03

Main Idea feel

Details ① quiet ② danger ③ protect

Conclusion farmers

STEP 04

1 No, I don't 　2 Yes, I do

09 Environment 42쪽

Animals Need Quiet Homes, Too

STEP 01

1 ① leave ② Ship ③ babies

2 ① F ② T

3 people, well-being

STEP 03

Main Idea pollution

Details ① near ② stressed ③ communicating

Conclusion affects

STEP 04

1 Yes, I do 2 No, I don't

10 Science 46쪽

Can Humans Make Diamonds?

STEP 01

1 ① diamonds ② nature ③ devices

2 ① F ② T

3 labs, industries

STEP 03

Main Idea man-made

Details ① natural ② cheaper ③ companies

Conclusion science

STEP 04

1 No, I don't 2 Yes, I do

11 Environment 50쪽

Food Waste Isn't Just about Food

STEP 01

1 ① grow ② wasted ③ burns

2 ① F ② T

3 Throwing away, many

STEP 03

Main Idea impact

Details ① resources ② food ③ gases

Conclusion waste

STEP 04

1 Yes, I do 2 No, I don't

12 Science 54쪽

Fake Germs, Real Protection

STEP 01

1 ① immune ② germs ③ weak

2 ① T ② F

3 Vaccines, sickness

STEP 03

Main Idea safe

Details ① weak ② remembers ③ faster

Conclusion protect

STEP 04

1 No, I don't 2 Yes, I do

13 Environment Environment — 58쪽

Save Water, Save the World!

STEP 01

1 ① water ② droughts ③ save

2 ① F ② T

3 Climate change, wisely

STEP 03

Main Idea find

Details ① dry ② affects ③ off

Conclusion simple

STEP 04

1 Yes, I do **2** No, I don't

14 Science — 62쪽

Can Robots Feel Emotions?

STEP 01

1 ① Robots ② faces ③ real

2 ① T ② T

3 emotions, understand

STEP 03

Main Idea human-like

Details ① respond ② feelings ③ code

Conclusion work

STEP 04

1 No, I don't **2** Yes, I do

15 Environment — 66쪽

Too Many Clothes, Too Much Waste

STEP 01

1 ① problem ② cheap ③ longer

2 ① T ② F

3 Fast fashion, pollution

STEP 03

Main Idea serious

Details ① throwing ② harms ③ eco-friendly

Conclusion How

STEP 04

1 Yes, I do **2** No, I don't

16 Science — 70쪽

No Driver, No Problem?

STEP 01

1 ① drivers ② tested ③ safer

2 ① T ② F

3 technology, rules

STEP 03

Main Idea concern

Details ① without ② travel ③ accidents

Conclusion testing

STEP 04

1 Yes, I do **2** No, I don't

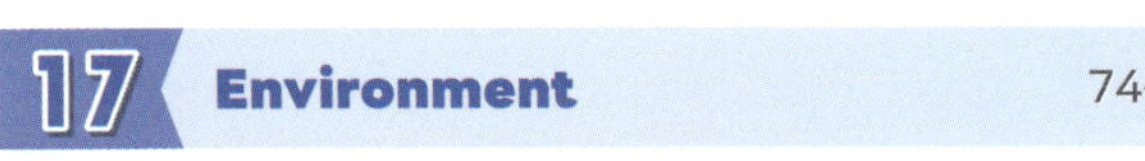

17   Environment   74쪽

The Earth Is Warming Too Fast

STEP 01

1 ① warming ② floods ③ forever

2 ① F ② T

3 faster, before

STEP 03

Main Idea quickly

Details ① decade ② Fires ③ disappear

Conclusion protect

STEP 04

1 No, I don't   **2** Yes, I do

18   Science   78쪽

Smarter Arms and Legs

STEP 01

1 ① machine ② real ③ thinking

2 ① F ② T

3 Bionic, smarter

STEP 03

Main Idea limbs

Details ① signals ② control ③ less

Conclusion hope

STEP 04

1 Yes, I do   **2** No, I don't

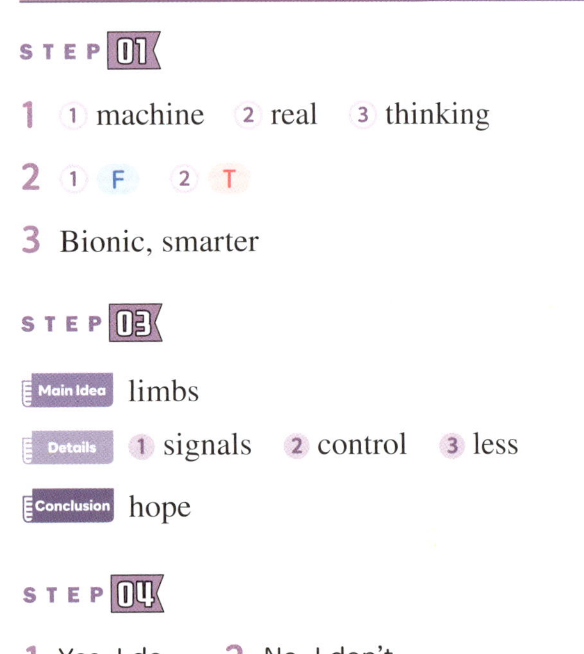

19   Environment   82쪽

Fun Festivals, Big Trash

STEP 01

1 ① festivals ② waste ③ plastic

2 ① T ② T

3 trash, eco-friendly

STEP 03

Main Idea create

Details ① festival ② fewer ③ visitors

Conclusion important

STEP 04

1 No, I don't   **2** Yes, I do

20   Science   86쪽

Is Nuclear Power Worth the Risk?

STEP 01

1 ① Nuclear ② carbon ③ waste

2 ① T ② F

3 clean, risks

STEP 03

Main Idea energy

Details ① accidents ② high ③ clean

Conclusion climate change

STEP 04

1 Yes, I do   **2** No, I don't

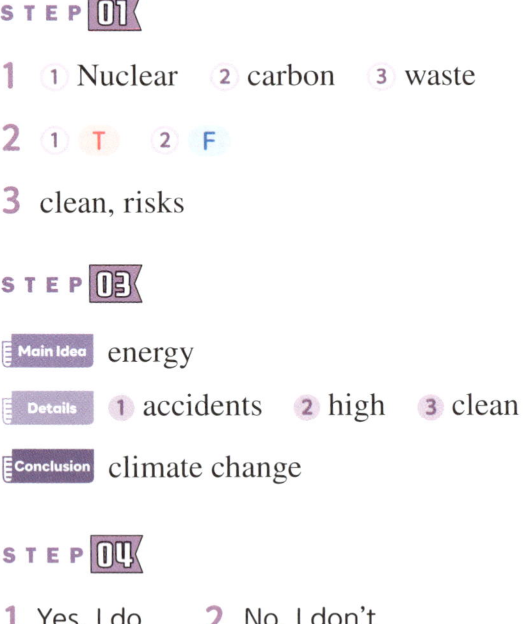

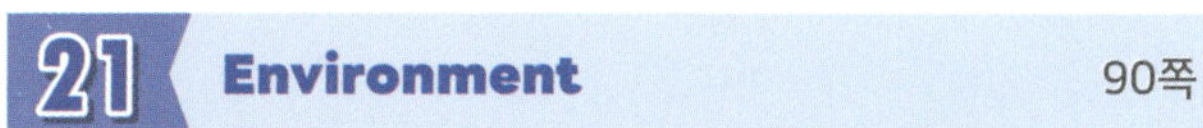

21 Environment — 90쪽

The Truth about Bottled Water

STEP 01

1 ① bottled ② oil ③ safer

2 ① F ② T

3 tap, health

STEP 03

Main Idea environmental

Details ① resources ② plastics ③ reduce

Conclusion actions

STEP 04

1 Yes, I do **2** No, I don't

22 Science — 94쪽

Should Kids Use AI for Homework?

STEP 01

1 ① help ② homework ③ own

2 ① T ② F

3 skills, AI

STEP 03

Main Idea small

Details ① students ② avoid ③ weaker

Conclusion wisely

STEP 04

1 No, I don't **2** Yes, I do

23 Environment — 98쪽

Fast Delivery, Big Problem

STEP 01

1 ① waste ② packages ③ Earth

2 ① F ② T

3 shopping, pollution

STEP 03

Main Idea harms

Details ① creates ② Delivery ③ worse

Conclusion environment

STEP 04

1 Yes, I do **2** No, I don't

24 Science — 102쪽

Smart Farms: The Future of Farming

STEP 01

1 ① sensors ② itself ③ insects

2 ① T ② F

3 farmers, all year

STEP 03

Main Idea year

Details ① technology ② automatically ③ pesticide

Conclusion farming

STEP 04

1 No, I don't **2** Yes, I do

25 Environment — The Truth about Palm Oil (106쪽)

STEP 01

1 ① palm oil ② destroys ③ labels

2 ① F ② T

3 without, protect

STEP 03

Main Idea hurts

Details ① rainforests ② disappeared ③ ingredient

Conclusion wildlife

STEP 04

1 Yes, I do   **2** No, I don't

26 Science — New Glasses, New Possibilities (110쪽)

STEP 01

1 ① glasses ② AR ③ work

2 ① F ② T

3 more, daily life

STEP 03

Main Idea change

Details ① images ② daily ③ wearable devices

Conclusion everyday life

STEP 04

1 Yes, I do   **2** No, I don't

27 Environment — Sand in Danger (114쪽)

STEP 01

1 ① sand ② without ③ oil

2 ① F ② T

3 demand, enough

STEP 03

Main Idea daily life

Details ① glass ② more ③ permission

Conclusion Saving

STEP 04

1 Yes, I do   **2** No, I don't

28 Science — Holes under Our Feet (118쪽)

STEP 01

1 ① sinkholes ② radar ③ moving

2 ① F ② T

3 find, happen

STEP 03

Main Idea methods

Details ① empty ② satellites ③ hole

Conclusion protect

STEP 04

1 No, I don't   **2** Yes, I do

29 Environment 122쪽

Clean and Check before Recycling

STEP 01

1 ① recycled ② dirty ③ plastic

2 ① F ② T

3 Recycling, responsible

STEP 03

Main Idea recycled

Details ① materials ② clean ③ check

Conclusion home

STEP 04

1 Yes, I do   **2** No, I don't

30 Science 126쪽

Diet Shots vs. Healthy Habits

STEP 01

1 ① weight ② hormone ③ food

2 ① T ② F

3 side effects, habits

STEP 03

Main Idea obesity

Details ① lose ② less ③ sick

Conclusion exercising

STEP 04

1 Yes, I do   **2** No, I don't

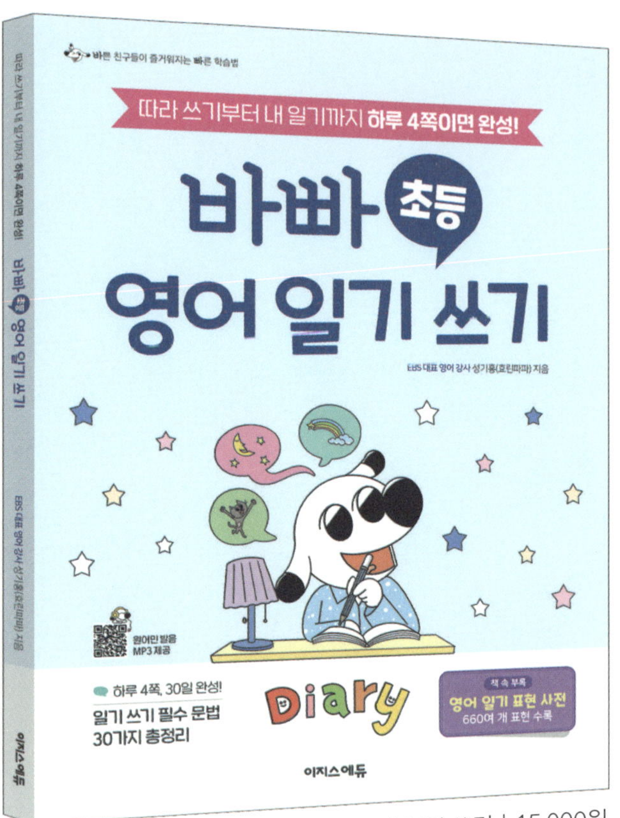

바빠 초등 영어 일기 쓰기 | 15,000원

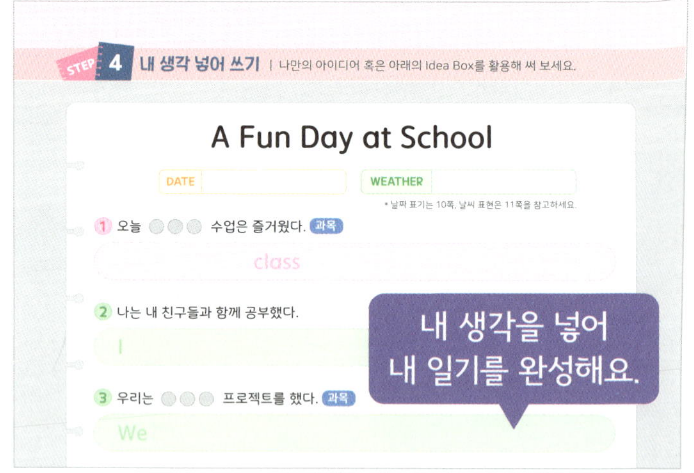